JUN FAN GUNG FU

SEEKING THE PATH OF JEET KUNE DO
by
Kevin R. Seaman

JUN FAN GUNG FU
SEEKING THE PATH OF JEET KUNE DO

by
Kevin R. Seaman

© 1999 HNL Publishing/Kevin R. Seaman. All rights reserved.

No part of this publication may be reproduced, stored in a retrieval system, or transmitted in any form or by any means electronic, mechanical, recording, or otherwise, without the prior written permission of the publisher.

ISBN: 0-9531766-2-2

HNL PUBLISHING

5918 Fort Hamilton Parkway
Brooklyn
New York-11219-USA

Disclaimer – Neither the author nor the publisher assumes any responsibility in any manner whatsoever for any injury which may occur by reading or following the instructions herein.

Consult your physician before following any of the activities.

(Cover photo by Wayne Hansen.)

THE AUTHOR KEVIN R. SEAMAN

CONTENTS

LESSON ONE   21
    JUN FAN GUNG FU'S FOOTWORK

LESSON TWO   37
    FOOTWORK AND MOBILITY TRAINING DRILLS

LESSON THREE   47
    OFFENSIVE HAND TECHNIQUES

LESSON FOUR   73
    BASIC FOCUS GLOVE FEED DRILLS

LESSON FIVE   81
    DEFENSIVE HAND TECHNIQUES

LESSON SIX   95
    SIMULTANEOUS BLOCK AND STRIKE

LESSON SEVEN   105
    BASIC KICKING TECHNIQUES

LESSON EIGHT   125
    JUN FAN TRAPPING

LESSON NINE   145
    JKD'S FIVE WAYS OF ATTACK DRILLS

LESSON TEN   169
    JUN FAN AND JEET KUNE DO TERMINOLOGY

Dedicated to the spirit and memory of Sigung Bruce Lee, a man who has inspired millions.

Also to Sifu Dan Inosanto, the man who has kept the flame of Jeet Kune Do alive, an extraordinary teacher and true genius in his field.

He has kept the art, philosophy, teachings and techniques of Sigung Lee alive, true to form and integrity, and well protected and preserved for the future.

ACKNOWLEDGEMENTS

My road to personal development has been a very long, unique and interesting journey. Over the years I have had many people and experiences that have helped teach, influence and guide me to become the person I am today. One of the things I am most grateful for is the generosity of so many individuals and the time and patience they had when sharing their knowledge with myself and others. I would like to thank anyone who may have influenced me. I would especially like to thank my teachers.

THREE MAJOR INFLUENCES IN MY PERSONAL MARTIAL ARTS DEVELOPMENT. (LEFT TO RIGHT) SIFU FRANCIS FONG, SIFU DAN INOSANTO AND AJARN CHAI SIRISUTE

To Sifu Dan Inosanto, I thank you from the depth of my heart and soul. In addition to teaching me unselfishly nearly every aspect I needed to understand the system of Jun Fan Gung Fu and the art and philosophy of Jeet Kune Do (as well as introducing me to many other different martial arts and cultures.) You have taught me to look within and to always respect myself and others. Your teaching methodology and ability can only be shadowed by your generosity, humility, and genuine concern for those around you. In addition to being an extraordinary teacher. you are truly one of the most amazing individuals I have ever met.

To Sifu Francis Fong, I am truly in your debt. Your insight into the foundational structure and function of Wing Chun and Jeet Kune Do has been a major influence on myself and many others as we've searched for improvement throughout the years. Your strength and sensitivity are absolutely phenomenal. You are one of the most gifted teachers I have ever met. I also want you to know that your personal compassion and friendship have always meant more to me than you can realize, way beyond what I could ever convey in words.

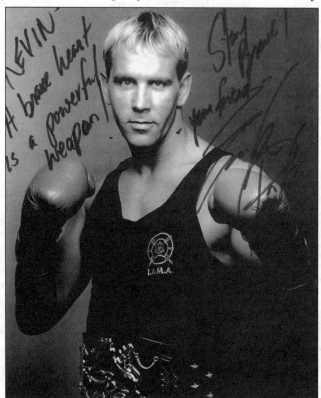

ERIK PAULSON – JKD INSTRUCTOR AND LIGHT HEAVYWEIGHT CHAMPION OF THE WORLD IN SHOOT WRESTLING

To Ajarn Chai Sirisute, your training has guided me to understand the importance of being physically conditioned and how to dig deep to accomplish the things we want. You have helped me to strengthen my heart and my mind by teaching me the discipline needed to develop and condition my body. Most of all you have taught me as much about myself as you have about martial arts. I thank you sir.

To Mr. Erik Paulson, my grappling mentor. You have been an inspiration to me, always encouraging me to improve and develop myself. Your personality, sense of humor, and imagination are unique. Thank you for all your help and guidance.

To all my other teachers in and outside the JKD family who have helped me along the way, thank you for all you have shared with me; you have all had an influence on me.

To my parents Jack and Nancy Seaman for their unending love and support in all I have attempted and accomplished. Thank you for all you have taught me about life. Although when I was younger it may not have seemed as though I was paying attention at times. You are one of the most important influences I've had in my life. Thank you for giving us a wonderful, caring home and loving environment to grow up in. Your interest in my personal character development and life direction played a major role in who I am today. I love you both very much.

To my amor, Cathy Gregg, my friend, my love, my training partner, and confidant. Thank you for all of your love, caring, positive energy, encouragement, and guidance; you're the most remarkable woman I've ever known; you've captured my heart.

To my peers and fellow students, thank you for allowing me to grow with you and all the hours we have all dedicated to each other's self improvement. Continue to believe in yourself, keep your goals alive, and take action to accomplish those goals, stay on the path of constant and never-ending improvement and most important never, never give up!

To my students, thank you for your dedication and discipline for without you I would not continue to grow.

To Bill Gebhardt, you are a great representation of what I have taught you over the years and your respect, loyalty and friendship have always been greatly appreciated. You have become an excellent teacher of the martial arts. Having always been like a son to me, I am extremely proud to see your many accomplishments and to see what a great person you have turned out to be.

To Alan Gutchess, who has stood by my side through the years and helped me with the demonstrations for the photographs in this book, thank you for all your friendship, help and devotion.

To Erik Russell, who has also been like a son to me. I am very proud of all of your accomplishments and success both in and out of the martial arts. Thank you for helping me with the ring portion and other photographs.

To Chad Engst, a man who's heart is as big as his gigantic frame. Your warmth and respect have always been very much appreciated. Thank you for your help with the photographic portion of the book and the hours of computer work with the text. Many thanks to Jim Brault for writing the foreword and helping to inspire me to write this book.

My thanks to photographers Larry Duran and Jim Hughes. It was fun.

Lastly to those of you who are seeking the path, thank you for taking the time and interest to improve yourself by reading this book. Always keep an open mind, a compassionate spirit, help others and of course, keep your hands up!

DAN INOSANTO AND SENIOR STUDENT AND AUTHOR KEVIN R. SEAMAN
(Photo by Markus Boesch)

ABOUT THE AUTHOR

Kevin R. Seaman began his martial arts training in 1970 in Southern California in Choy Li Fut Gung Fu under Sifu Ken Yue.

In the 1970s, Sifu Seaman actively participated in amateur boxing at the Los Angeles' Main Street Gym. While researching different training methods. he started training in Filipino Martial Arts in 1976. He has reached instructor level in six different martial arts systems.

Kevin Seaman is a senior student and Upstate NY representative for Dan Inosanto and is one of the few people in the Northeast authorized by Dan Inosanto to teach Bruce Lee's Jun Fan Gung Fu and the art and philosophy of Jeet Kune Do. He is one of a handful of selected individuals to hold a Full Instructor's credential under Sifu Inosanto in Jun Fan Gung Fu /Jeet Kune Do and in the Filipino Martial Arts. He also received a Full Instructor ranking in Jeet Kune Do by Sifu Tim Tackett in 1991.

Mr. Seaman has been involved on a regional, national and international level in full contact stick fighting and forms competition. In 1992, he competed on the US Team at the World Escrima, Kali, Arnis Championships in Manila, Philippines.

Sifu Seaman was certified by Master Surachai Sirisute as an instructor in Thai Boxing and appointed as New York state representative for the Thai Boxing Association USA in 1989.

In addition to teaching Thai Boxing classes at his academy, Sifu Seaman also teaches a credit physical education class in both Thai Boxing and Jun Fan Gung Fu, Art and Philosophy of Jeet Kune Do at Cornell University.

Sifu Seaman became a certified instructor in 1992 in Wing Chun Gung Fu under Sifu Francis Fong and New York state representative for the Francis Fong Academy of Atlanta, Georgia.

Kevin Seaman recently received his Instructor's Certification in Combat Submission Grappling under the guidance of Light heavy weight World Champion Shoot wrestler Mr. Erik Paulson of Los Angeles, California.

Kevin Seaman has taught the martial arts on a vocational level to hundreds of students of all ages for over 25 years.

FOREWORD

Just for a moment I want you to imagine something. Imagine that it were possible for you to study with the most gifted martial arts masters available, regardless of where they lived, how much it would cost, and even if they were living or deceased. During the course of your studying with these incredible teachers, imagine further that all of your training was one-on-one; it was just you and them. Now, imagine that no subject was taboo. That any question you asked would be answered, and any hint or piece of advice that would help make you a better martial artist would be shared with you. Finally, imagine that during the course of all these training sessions, you took meticulous notes that accurately chronicled the techniques, drills and insights you would have gleaned from studying with these masters.

If all of that were possible, I dare say that it would not be much different than what you now hold in your hands. Sifu Kevin Seaman's book is a wealth of information gleaned from years of study, teaching and application. Through it you will be introduced to Bruce Lee's style – Jun Fan Gung Fu, and to the art and philosophy of Jeet Kune Do in a way that makes perfect sense. Each section is broken down into easily digestible parts to be consumed as quickly or as slowly as you desire. It is a feast for both the intellect and the body.

To stimulate your mind, each section is filled with explanations behind how, why and when various approaches and techniques work. To challenge your body, each section is also overflowing with drills and training regimens to help you put those concepts to the test.

Throughout it all, Sifu Kevin is right there with you, explaining each step in clear, easy to understand language. It's like having a personal instructor by your side all the time. He'll also give you the kind of suggestions and tips that just don't come from anything but years of trial and error and seeing what does and doesn't work – it is a knowledge culled from generations of gifted martial artists all striving to be their best, sharing with their peers and students in an effort to raise everyone's skill level.

You have made an excellent investment by buying this book, and Kevin

Seaman has done a commendable job sharing the techniques, concepts and philosophy of a great man and martial artist, Bruce Lee. I wish you well in your training.
  Jim Brault
Martial artist and author 'Lessons from the Masters: Seven Keys to Peak Performance and Inner Peace'

WHAT IS...?
JUN FAN GUNG FU

Bruce Lee's composite method of Martial Arts evolved through research, thought and development, using highly efficient core methods from different Martial Arts systems. These core methods were developed into four sections: Wing Chun (Lee Jun Fan Method), Kick boxing (Lee Jun Fan Method), Chinese & Western Boxing and Grappling & Chin Na. Because of his research and development. Sijo Lee's art was constantly changing. The Jun Fan Martial Arts of 1964 looked somewhat different than 1965 and 1966, 1970, etc.

JEET KUNE DO

Bruce Lee was constantly searching to find a common thread blend of Martial Arts that fit him and allowed the personal expression. As he revised his approach, concepts and principles from Martial Arts were adopted, absorbed and applied to his Jun Fan Method. As he added, he also simplified, carving off the unwanted Material to meet his personal needs. This process evolved into an individualized way of applying these principles and thoughts, which eventually became the art, science & philosophy of Jeet Kune Do. Sijo (founder) Lee realized that Jun Fan Gung-Fu confined his application of concepts and principles to a singular method. restraining his JKD from total freedom and truth, as he defined it. The Jeet Kune Do Method of applying specific principles and concepts could and did apply to many Martial Arts movement systems.

Therefore, JKD is not Wing Chun. Kali. Kickboxing, or a combination of various Martial Arts systems. but can be found in part or applied to these systems and many others. Because concepts and principles are universal, they cannot be confined to, or contained in, only one method. Bruce Lee continued his revisions until his demise in 1973. Only three people were ever certified as instructors by Sijo Bruce Lee. They were Taky Kimura, James Lee and Dan Inosanto.

On March 27, 1981, Jun Fan Gung-Fu/Jeet Kune Do was inducted into the Kuoshu Federation of the Republic of China, recognizing it as a legitimate Martial Art.

The above was written and compiled by Sifu Kevin R. Seaman

"Jeet Kune Do favors formlessness so that it can assume all forms and since Jeet Kune Do has no style, it can fit in with all styles. As a result, Jeet Kune Do utilizes all ways and is bound by none and, likewise, uses any techniques or means which serve its end."
Sigung Bruce Lee

LESSON 1
JUN FAN GUNG FU'S FOOTWORK AND MOBILITY

Footwork and mobility are an essential part of the foundation of Jun Fan. Good footwork means having good balance in action. It allows you the mobility to close the distance effectively, avoid punishment and develop explosive hitting power. The one who controls the distance, can better control his opponent. Footwork in Jun Fan Gung Fu focuses on the Jeet Kune Do premise of simplification, using a minimum of movement for a maximum effect.

To be able to apply footwork effectively you must work on your personal development in this area. To be effective you must be proficient at each type of footwork and be able to express it, both individually and in combination, fluently at the exact instant each component is needed, this is accomplished through total freedom of expression. Freedom of expression comes from the development of one's self knowledge. The martial arts is a discipline, and like many other disciplines the martial arts demand self knowledge. In order to develop one's Jeet Kune Do one must develop their self knowledge.

Below are a few types of footwork used in Jun Fan. Some are a combination of the different basic components. Once you are able to smoothly perform each type, drill the basics until they become part of you. Work your footwork drills until you are able to use them without consciously having to think about what you are doing.

1. **The Bai-jong Stance** – On Guard Position
2. **The Step and Slide** (a short to mid-range advance and retreat)
3. **The Side Step** – (Step and Slide right and left)
4. **Triangular Step**

5. Slide and Step or Standard Shuffle (a long range advance and retreat)
6. Pendulum (advance and retreat in one motion)
7. Step and Shuffle (an extended, long range advance and retreat)
8. The Push step
9. Circling (right and left)

THE ON GUARD POSITION BAI-JONG STANCE

The On Guard Position is the foundational premise from which all footwork in Jun Fan begins. For the purpose of this book we will perform all our techniques from a right lead stance. This will be based on our right side being our strong side, using the JKD concept of keeping our strong side forward. To begin, the lead toe should line up with the rear heel with the feet about shoulder width apart. Your lead foot should be turned inward about 35°- 45° to protect your centerline and groin area. Your rear foot should also be turned about 45° with the heel slightly raised. Keep your lead hand in alignment with your centerline, relaxed, yet ready to strike or defend.

The lead hand known as the mon sao or inquisitive hand defends the face, throat, chest, stomach, and groin. The lead elbow acts as a guard to protect the ribs and mid-section and should be stationed a distance of one and a half to two fists from the body. The rear hand should be attentively positioned below the jaw. This is your wu sao or protecting hand, it protects your head, mid-section, and groin. The rear elbow is kept near the body to guard the rib area. While in the On Guard position, your shoulders should be slightly raised, but relaxed with your chin slightly lowered to meet your shoulders half way. Check your structure in front of a mirror. Your body should be able to rock forward and back by raising and lowering your heel, and shifting your weight. Feel your balance, rock back and forth, sway or slip from side to side.

THE STEP AND SLIDE ADVANCE AND RETREAT

From the right lead On Guard Position, the first basic we'll cover is the Step and Slide. The step and slide is a short range footwork used to get you in and out of range quickly.

When you step forward, step with your lead foot first and slide your rear foot the same distance as your step, ending in the Bai-jong On guard position. To retreat, first step, with your rear foot, then slide your lead foot the same distance as your retreating step. Be sure not to take too big a step. This will limit your ability to move. If you need more distance step and slide twice. The step and slide is the key to mid-range (punching) and trapping.

SIDE STEP – STEP AND SLIDE
(RIGHT AND LEFT)

To side step an opponent's straight line attack such as a lead jab or front kick, use the step and slide right or left. To step and slide right move your lead foot by stepping to the right and sliding your left foot in the same direction. Be sure to move at least one shoulder width and finish in the Bai-jong stance. To move left always move your rear foot first by stepping to the left and sliding your right in the same direction and end in the Bai-jong stance.

Your weight should float without too much weight on one foot or the other. Regardless of whether you're in a right or left lead, when you move to the right always move your right foot first. As you step shift your weight, moving your head in the direction of your step. When you move to the left always move your left foot first and then slide your right.

TRIANGULAR STEP

The triangular step is a step and slide done at a 45° angle. We will address its usage in moving forward. The triangular step can be used to zone inside and away from an attack. (Rear round Kick), to bob under an attack (ex. left cross), or slip an attack while moving in. The triangular step can be used to change the direction of your lead or with the pivot step to circle out, changing the direction of your attack.

ABOVE: TRIANGULAR STEP USING THE REAR BODY SHOT

BELOW: TRIANGULAR STEP USING THE LEAD HAND SHOT

SLIDE AND STEP (OR STANDARD SHUFFLE)

The slide and step shuffle is a long range footwork maneuver. I refer to this as the standard shuffle. The strength of this type of shuffle is that you can cover a substantial distance forward or backward very quickly. This shuffle will get you out of kicking range as you retreat from an aggressive attack. It is also very effective at closing the distance while increasing the power and range of your lead kick. The weakness of the slide and step shuffle is in its commitment. It can be jammed by an opponent if he times your advance.

The mechanics of the slide and step are simple. To advance slide your rear foot forward, behind your lead foot, and step forward with your lead foot ending in the Bai-jong stance On Guard position. Your balance should be stable, both during and upon completion. To retreat slide your lead foot back, ending in front of the your rear foot and step back with your rear foot ending once again in the On Guard Position. You should move naturally, lightly shuffling on the balls of your feet, close to the floor. Slide rhythmically just above the surface but don't hop up and down.

JUN FAN GUNG FU

PENDULUM SHUFFLE

The Pendulum is a variation of the standard shuffle. It's used to apply various lead kicks from a safe distance, while moving in and out of range quickly and efficiently. It is also instrumental in the application of many stop kicks which intercept and stop your opponent's attack. The Pendulum Shuffle covers a

shorter distance than the standard shuffle. As you move, your head stays in the same area while your lower body moves much like the pendulum of a clock. This makes the pendulum less telegraphic and more difficult to detect when executed properly.

JUN FAN GUNG FU

PENDULUM SIDE KICK APPLICATION

STEP AND SHUFFLE

This is a composite of the step and slide and the slide and step shuffle. Bruce Lee referred to this as the Quick advance. To do the step and shuffle first step forward with your lead foot then slide your rear foot forward projecting your body in the same direction as you shuffle. The short step allows a greater distance to be covered and allows for a little more quickness and ease of movement in your advance. When retreating use the slide and step shuffle, unless the extra distance is absolutely needed.

SEEKING THE PATH OF JEET KUNE DO

STEP AND SHUFFLE DRILL USING THE KICK SHIELD TO LEARN TO CLOSE THE DISTANCE

THE PUSH STEP

The push step is a fully committed, medium distance method used to advance or retreat quickly. In advancing the push step is used to explode forward, while attacking simultaneously. The power is most efficiently used. for example when your lead straight punch Chung Chuie or lead thrust kick lands before your weight lands on your recovering foot. This will drive your force into the target rather than into the ground. The push step can also be used to effectively apply the lead finger jab Bil Gee or back fist Qua Chuie with blinding speed.

CIRCLING RIGHT AND LEFT

Circling comprises two directions of the basic four found in all footwork. Circling is composed of lateral footwork or side stepping and pivotal footwork. From a right lead stance move your lead foot first while shifting to the right, then take a little larger sliding step with your left foot. By pivoting on the ball of your right foot, your left foot will make a sweeping semi-circle. What you want to accomplish is to move safely and deliberately away from the attack without excess motion. Be sure not to cross your feet when stepping and always be ready to snap out the lead hand attack or counter. When circling left (from the right lead) step with your rear foot first, then shift your weight, drawing your right foot toward you. This maneuver is more difficult, but safer if your opponent is also in a right lead because you will avoid the rear hand attack and move to his back.

SLIPPING AN ATTACK

Slipping an attack requires skill and timing. In a right Bai-Jong stance face the mirror and visualize a committed straight line punch being thrown at your face. To slip your right, pivot your rear foot to your right bringing your left shoulder forward. As you slip right, your head should align with your right foot. Return to your ready position and repeat your slip. To slip left, pivot your lead foot to the left while shifting your weight slightly to your rear foot. When you slip left your head should align with your left foot. Once you've developed a degree of comfort and confidence in your movement, apply your slip to a lead hand straight line attack. Work slow at first. For safety purposes your partner should wear a boxing glove and you should wear a mouthpiece.

BOB OR DUCK

A bob and a duck are similar. When you bob you bend your waist while bending your knees slightly. A duck is performed by bending mostly at the knees. Both a bob and a duck are best used when evading a committed attack to your head.

BOB AND WEAVE

The bob and weave is a combination of a bob and a slip. To bob and weave to the right, bob down slip right and then bob back up. Your head should make a "U" from left to right. To bob and weave left, reverse the process. When you apply a bob and weave always move into the attack as you weave. This will put you on the outside of the attack and in an optimal position for you to counter. Notice how your body will naturally wind up.

To bob and weave a rear cross or rear hook from a matched stance, your body will wind up, ready to deliver the lead hook/rear cross counter. To bob a lead hook your body should be spring loaded to unleash a rear cross, lead hook combination. As you improve throw a body hook as you weave and increase your application of follow up combinations.

SHOULDER ROLL

The shoulder roll is an evasive technique used to defend against a rear cross or rear straight punch to your head. As your opponent steps in with a jab/cross, parry the jab with your rear pak sao and roll your shoulder while shifting your weight back. Be sure to keep your chin tucked next to your shoulder, raising your shoulder slightly. Your lead arm should be bent and held close to cover the body. Your rear hand is held in the guard position. As your opponent retracts his cross, rock forward, back into your Bai-Jong stance while delivering a rear cross. Another way of applying the shoulder roll is with a simultaneous low lead kick. This can be done with a low side stop kick to the shin or a low round kick to the inside thigh/knee area or the groin.

FOOTWORK
KEY POINTS TO REMEMBER

1. Maintain your balance at all times.

2. Combine and vary different footwork patterns while shadow boxing. Begin your warm-up with 2- 3 rounds of shadow boxing, three minutes in length with a one minute rest.

3. Train footwork with speed and agility in mind. Don't be flat footed, stay on the balls of your feet when moving, and stay relaxed.

4. "Distance" in fighting can be defined as the spatial relationship between you and your opponent. The distance one tries to maintain is known as the fighting measure.

5. The one who controls the distance, can better control his opponent.

6. Footwork in Jun Fan focuses on simplification with a minimum of movement and a maximum effect.

7. By constantly moving and adjusting the distance you are able to:
a. Cause your opponent's attack to miss, avoiding punishment. Move only enough to evade the attack, then counter.
b. Control and find the correct distance to launch your attack with explosive power.
c. Disrupt your opponent's strategy or plan of action.

8. Moving is used as a means of defense, a means of deception, a means of securing proper distance for an attack, and a way of conserving energy. In short: The essence of fighting is the art of moving.

SIFU FRANCIS FONG DEMONSTRATING WITH KEVIN SEAMAN AT ONE OF HIS SEMINARS

The goal of the martial arts is not for the destruction of an opponent, but rather for self-growth and self-perfection. The practice of a martial art should be a practice of love – for the preservation of life, for the preservation of body, and for the preservation of family and friends.
– Sifu Dan Inosanto

LESSON 2
FOOTWORK AND MOBILITY TRAINING AND DEVELOPMENT DRILLS

In this section I will address a few ways to develop agility in footwork through various active drills used in Jun Fan Gung Fu. Practice the drills with your partner at the beginning of your training sessions. This will help program you to use your footwork optimally throughout the rest of your workout.

If you have access to a boxing ring, work your footwork in the ring. The matted canvas surface is an incredible strength and endurance builder. Jumping rope is also a great tool for increasing your leg strength, agility, timing, tempo and co-ordination. Jump rope on a mat whenever possible. In order for a student to become proficient in the application of any footwork they must cultivate certain qualities or attributes and practice the basic technical skills until they become natural. Work your footwork with the goal becoming relaxed, yet "alive" on your feet. At the tail of the section are 3 of many training drills which will aid you by increasing your strength, co-ordination, agility, balance, and muscular endurance. If possible do these exercises on a matted surface as well. Be sure you're warmed up and well stretched before you begin any type of training.

To supplement your footwork training cross train in the weight room with low weight, high repetition leg strengthening exercises such as leg press, medium squats, quad extensions, and leg curls. Consult a qualified trainer for proper form when doing anything you're not totally familiar with. To improve your endurance investigate blending mountain biking, stair stepper, wind sprints and interval training into your cross training regiment. Bruce Lee believed in cross training long before it was popular amongst most sports trainers and martial artists.

THE FIGHTING MEASURE

A major principle in Jeet Kune Do is to control the distance between you and your opponent. This distance is referred to as the spatial relationship or 'fighting measure.' Your distance should be maintained, so your opponent must move forward in order to be in range to land an attack. As your opponent moves in, you will need to move back or side step in order to maintain a safe distance. If he retreats you should stay with him, maintaining your 'fighting measure.' You should be able to move swiftly in any direction to evade even the most aggressive opponent and elude almost any blow. Your body should always work to be in the optimum position to deliver a skilful and immediate counter or take any opportunity to attack the moment your opponent is unguarded, out of time or unbalanced.

HEEL TO TOE SWAY BACK

Square off with your partner at punching distance. As your partner jabs, sway back, avoiding his jab. Then immediately return your jab as you sway forward. Your partner snaps away from your lead attack and the cycle continues. Do this drill in a 3 count. As you improve. move around applying your step and slide or circling footwork.

SEEKING THE PATH OF JEET KUNE DO

STEP AND SLIDE MIRROR DRILL

This drill can be done in a matched stance or an unmatched stance. Be sure you are outside of kicking range, so your opponent would have to step in order to kick, punch, or grab you. As your partner moves, mirror his movement by moving with him. Start out slowly at first by using single motions. When he moves forward, you move back. When he moves back, you move forward. If he sidesteps left, you follow by moving right. And if he moves right, you move to the left. This drill will help to improve your ability to read your opponent's intention. As you improve, alter the speed and tempo, as you initiate your movement.

STEP AND SLIDE FORWARD/ STEP AND SLIDE BACK

The step and slide forward and back drill will help you maintain and gauge your distance while in punching range. This drill will also introduce you to the concept of training in three counts. Training in three counts is beneficial because it allows you to experience attack and counter as well as basic rhythm timing. As you square off with your partner just outside of punching range, step and slide forward while delivering a lead jab or straight punch.

As you move, your partner reads your motion and step and slides back with a lead or rear pak sao. Immediately after his parry. he step and slides forward. returning a counter punch. As your partner moves forward, you move back, maintaining the fighting measure parry with your lead o rear hand. You then step and slide forward with your counter punch. As your partner responds, you've completed the first cycle. Your partner would now initiate the first motion of the next 3 count cycle, as you continue through the series. 10 sets of three are recommended in both right and left leads. Later this drill can be done in a matched or unmatched lead, hitting or countering high or low and varying your speed and timing.

STANDARD SHUFFLE – DISTANCE DRILL

This basic drill will help you to apply your footwork to avoid a committed kicking attack. As your partner feeds you a shuffle side kick or a step and shuffle side kick to your midsection, retreat staying just out of range of his kick. Try to read the distance so that the kick comes within inches or just brushes you. Don't block, evade. The objective of the kicker is to make it hard to read the distance. Start slow at first, without a lot of power behind your kick. As your ability to read the distance improves. your partner should vary the speed and distance of his commitment.

STANDARD SHUFFLE BACK/ STEP AND SLIDE FORWARD

Practice this drill first as a solo drill. Standard shuffle backward, as if you are avoiding a kick. Then immediately step and slide forward while delivering a lead straight punch. This can also be done with a jab/cross as you step and slide. When you jab/cross, step as you jab and slide your rear foot as you cross. Drop your weight slightly and rotate your hip and shoulder behind your cross. Always maintain your balance. Be aware of the alignment of your powerlines and be sure to protect your groin as you step in.

Practice this drill by applying the push step forward after you shuffle back, as well. To apply this to a partner drill. use the mirror concept from the first drill we covered earlier in the chapter. As your partner shuffles forward, shuffle back maintaining your distance. You then step and slide or push step forward and your partner step and slides back. Reverse your roles as you continue the cycle.

STRENGTHENING DRILLS

STRENGTHENING DRILLS WILL HELP YOU DEVELOP EXPLOSIVE POWER WHEN KICKING

ROCKER SHUFFLE

To begin the rocker shuffle start with the Bai-jong stance. Push off with your rear foot by using the ball of your foot and project your body forward. When your lead foot makes contact with the ground immediately push off with the ball of your lead foot projecting your body backward shifting your weight back to your rear foot.

Repeat the forward and back rocking shuffle while keeping your momentum in motion, remembering to stay on the balls of your feet as you move. Start with one set 3 minutes in length, progress to two 5 minute sets after a few weeks and eventually increase to one 15-20 minute set. Do this at least twice a week as your warm up before training.

SINGLE LEG HOPS

Affectionately known as "calf burners" these will strengthen your calf muscles quicker than any exercise I've ever seen. Be cautious if you have had any knee injuries as squatting type exercises can aggravate or prolong a chronic or acute knee injury.

To begin, grab your partner's right leg with your left hand and let them grab your right leg with their left hand. Then grab your partner's right hand with the arm wrestling grip to help you balance. As you both begin to hop on the balls of your feet coordinate the tempo with your partner allowing your movement to be synchronised. As you reach your peak, about 30 seconds for most people switch legs and work the other side. I'm sure you'll find two 30-45 second sets twice a week to be very effective at building the spring in your calves and feet.

SQUAT JUMPS

I've found that squat jumps are best done at the conclusion of your workout. These will do wonders for your kicking power as well as helping to develop explosive footwork. I recommend you do these on a mat to help reduce the impact. Start with your feet a little more than shoulder width apart. While keeping your back slightly arched begin your squat. Be sure not to go any lower than a 30° inclining angle with your thigh. As your reach this point spring upward while swinging your arms toward the sky. When you land, continue down to your previous squat position and prepare to push On again.

As a variation you can to change your position from a right to a left lead squat after each jump. Continue this series of motions exploding upward with each repetition until a set of 30 is complete. As you improve build to 50 reps each time.

IN CONCLUSION:

The most important thing you can do to improve your footwork and develop it into smooth natural motion is practice and more practice. Before you can possibly use your footwork in sparring or in a real street situation it must become automatic. This can only be accomplished through repetition. Sifu Dan Inosanto has said to me, "When you get sick and tired of doing the same thing over and over, you've GOT IT!"

Start out slowly at first and build the pace of your intensity. Don't be flat-footed, feel the floor with the balls of your feet. Quick relaxed footwork is a matter of proper weight distribution and balance. Train footwork with speed and agility in mind. Remember, the one who controls the distance can better control his opponent.

In the words of Si-Gung Bruce Lee: "The essence of fighting is the art of moving." Develop the art with the goal to become your personal best.

QUESTIONS ABOUT FOOTWORK AND BODY MOTION

Q. Where should I look when sparring or faced with an opponent? Should I look in a person's eyes?

A. You should not look in the eyes. Fixing your attention on the opponent's eyes can be dangerous. This will tell you nothing about what they are going to do, and you may be easily fooled or psyched out. You should look at the body as a "T". The vertical line signifies the centreline, while the horizontal line runs from shoulder to shoulder. Watch the centre of the chest to help predicts how your opponent will move. In order for an opponent to punch you they must rotate, to kick with their lead they have to drop their rear shoulder. To kick with the rear leg the lead shoulder must drop as the other shoulder rotates into the kick. The whole body should be part of your peripheral focus.

Q. What type of shoes should I wear when I train?

A. Good question! Your shoes are very important. The best shoes for martial arts are training or court shoes or a shoe with a wide flat bottom. The advantage court shoes offer are good support and are designed for both forward and lateral movement. Some people prefer wrestling shoes, but be aware these offer little arch support.Stay away from running shoes. Running shoes are designed for running in a forward stride, heel to toe.

Q. Isn't a wide front or horsestance more stable then the Jun Fan stance? It seems like you're just jumping around.What about stability and balance?

A. One of the key points in Jun Fan Gung Fu is agility in footwork and controlling the gap between you and your opponent. Balance is absolutely essential, one should always maintain balance and stability in motion. To have stability however, does not mean you have to sink your weight low inhibiting your ability to move actively and nimbly. Your balance should be maintained at all times whether you are on your feet, on the mat or in the air.

SEEKING THE PATH OF JEET KUNE DO

DEMONSTRATING A ROUND OF JUN FAN KICKBOXING ON THE FOCUS GLOVES WITH JUN FAN INSTRUCTOR CATHY GREGG

"Sifu Bruce was constantly evolving. When I trained with him in 1964, he didn't possess the alive footwork that he later used. This came about through experimentation and constant practice."
– Sifu Dan Inosanto

LESSON 3
OFFENSIVE HAND TECHNIQUES

The most outstanding characteristics of Jun Fan's offensive hand techniques evolved thru the quest for maximum power and efficiency. Utilizing body torque and alignment, keyed with the application of non-telegraphic execution, Jun Fan's direction toward speed, power and effectiveness were truly the products of research and development.

Although the major contributors were Wing Chun Gung Fu and Western boxing, much of the concept of non-telegraphic efficiency was derived from Western fencing. Bruce Lee adopted a portion of the footwork and the principle of thrusting the hand on route to its destination before moving the body, as is done in foil fencing. If done correctly the JKD lead strike is extremely difficult to see coming, let alone block. Practice all your lead hand techniques within a wide range of combination attacks.

Add variety to your workout by hitting different target surfaces. For strength and power, hit a heavy bag, to work on your timing use a double end ball. To improve your speed and focus, strike a tennis ball hanging on a cord. This is a very inexpensive training tool that can be an inexhaustible source of challenge for any level of student. The two greatest training tools you can have at your disposal to help you develop your punching and striking ability are a large mirror to study your form, body mechanics and guard and a pair of focus mitts with an ambitious trainer or training partner attached to them.

If your community has a boxing gym, cross train with them whenever possible. Enter the gym with an empty cup and a thirst for learning. A boxing workout offers the martial artist an effective training approach, and will sharpen footwork, guard, punching skills and sparring ability.

Be sure to stay relaxed and work consistently on perfecting your form. Repetition and excellent form are the keys to quality. It doesn't matter how hard you hit, if you're sloppy, unrelaxed, off balance and unguarded a skilled opponent will hit you at will.

THE LEAD STRAIGHT PUNCH – "CHUNG CHUIE"

FRONT VIEW

SIDE VIEW

APPLICATION

The lead straight punch should be non-telegraphic in nature, and executed from a relaxed, ready posture. It should be straight or slightly angled to the target and use economy of motion, without any preparation. Relaxation is essential to develop a faster, more powerful punch.

Instead of coming from the shoulder or hip, the straight lead is thrown from the center of the body. The fist is vertical or turned slightly to a diagonal position with the palm side facing upward at an angle. To make a fist curl your fingers in. Now lay the thumb on the side across the first two fingers. Let your punch shoot out loosely and easily, your hand should be relaxed, until just before impact. Be sure the arm moves in a straight plane of motion with your wrist and elbow in alignment behind the fist. The fist should return along the same path with a slight elliptical motion at the extension.

The key to punching with power is shifting your weight. You never hit the person with your fist only, you hit them with your whole body! You should punch through the target, not at it.

The beauty of the straight lead is that it can be used effectively at both punching range and trapping range. The straight punch can be lead or rear. When thrown as a rear strike the body mechanics are essentially the same as the rear cross.

REAR STRAIGHT PUNCH – "HOU CHUNG CHUIE"

FRONT VIEW

SIDE VIEW

APPLICATION

Much like the lead straight punch, the rear chung chuie is thrown from the center of the body, with the fist in a vertical position. As with most punches, your punch should shoot out loosely and easily with your hand relaxed until just before impact. Rotate your knee, hip, and shoulder into the blow, while pivoting on the ball of your rear foot. Shift your weight forward and bend your rear knee, pointing it in the direction of your powerline, with your heel slightly raised.

LEAD SNAP PUNCH

The lead snap punch is a short range blow. It should be executed from a relaxed, ready position. Be sure to warm up well before you begin. The snap punch has some similarity to a straight punch, but is more of a jolt than a power shot. Start with your hand relaxed, as you shoot your hand out, extend your elbow completely, snapping your fist into the target diagonally. Be sure

FRONT VIEW

SIDE VIEW

APPLICATION

your fist is in a diagonal, not a vertical position. Because the snap punch is done at short range, your shoulder does not completely rotate as you hit. The penetration should be about 1-3 inches and your partner should feel a definite snap, as you hit the focus mitt.

THE LEAD JAB – "PING CHUIE"

FRONT VIEW

SIDE VIEW

APPLICATION

The lead jab is typically a long range punch used as a feeler to get a reaction, provoke an opening, set up a combination of attacks, or counter an oncoming opponent. It should be, as Jack Dempsey called it, "a jolt" not a poke. You want to explode your jab through your target. From the "on guard" position snap your jab out loosely with your hands relaxed.

As your jab extends, your chin is tucked into your shoulder, and your weight should shift forward, rotating your hip and shoulder into the punch. As with all punching techniques, at the point of contact your hand should clinch into a fist and your fist, elbow and shoulder should line up constituting a "power line" to the target. Always keep your rear hand up, either in a catch position in front of your chin or on your jaw, as if talking on the telephone. Keep your elbow in to protect your rib area.

Be sure to return your jab high, back in front of your face. Don't drop or row your jab after extension. If your jab does not return to the guard position, you will be very susceptible to a lead or rear counter.

To be sure you bring your jab back, have your partner check you with the flat of the mitt, following your jab back to the source. Work both single and double jab. Practice your jab until it is fast, light. and natural. Work on the focus mitt and have your partner flash the mitt randomly.

Accuracy. focus, and speed are your main objectives. Later, add explosive power. Remember that your body mechanics are essential to develop powerful hand techniques.

THE REAR CROSS

FRONT VIEW

The rear cross is a powerful straight line blow that capitalizes on body rotation behind the explosive penetration of a straight thrust. Classified as a major blow, the cross is often used in combination following a jab, lead straight or finger jab and preceding or following a lead hook. To learn the mechanics of of a cross you can use it in conjunction with the jab. As you throw the cross, draw your jab back to your jaw. Rotate your hip, knee and shoulder, while pivoting on the ball of your rear foot. Shift your weight 75 per cent forward and bend your rear knee, pointing it in the direction of your power line, with your heel slightly up.

Be sure to keep your elbow close to your body. Don't lift your elbow out as you punch. Keep the trajectory of your cross straight. On contact your fist. elbow and shoulder should line up with your foot and knee to complete your "power line." Upon completion or after contact, your fist will make a slightly elliptical motion and return to your jaw with your elbow in.

WRONG

SIDE VIEW

APPLICATION

KNUCKLE PUNCH – "CHOAP CHUIE"

The choap chuie is similar to ping chuie, but you strike with your 2nd knuckles. Choap chuie is used to hit soft tissue areas such as the throat and solar plexus. It can be applied vertically, horizontally. or diagonally with the palm facing up or down. It is usually done as a lead punch and is deep and penetrating.

FRONT VIEW

SIDE VIEW

APPLICATION

THE LEAD FINGER JAB – "BIL GEE"

The lead finger jab or Bil Gee (in Chinese) is the fastest, most efficient lead hand technique in "Jun Fan." With the extension of your fingers, it also provides you with a longer weapon. This was Sigung Bruce Lee's favorite primary opening attack, as it immediately disabled the opponent's visual capability. It was also frequently used by Lee in trapping during various (H.I.A.) hand immobilization attacks. The finger jab in "Jun Fan" is used like a fencer's foil. It should snap out loosely to the target, without any preparation. Your opponent's eyes and throat are the main target areas, so speed not power is most important. Work your finger jab for non-telegraphic speed and accuracy. Return immediately to the ready position.

You can practice the finger jab on a focus mitt for reflex and accuracy or on

SEEKING THE PATH OF JEET KUNE DO

FRONT VIEW

SIDE VIEW

APPLICATION

PRACTICE ON X-RAY PAPER

paper or X-ray film for lightness and depth. Always work your finger jab for a relaxed, fast touch. Be sure to keep your fingers curled slightly to avoid jamming them.

THE PALM JAB – "JERN"

The palm jab has similar mechanics to the jab but the striking surface is the palm heel. Your hand position can be vertical or slightly turned. Be sure to hit

FRONT VIEW

SIDE VIEW

APPLICATION

with the heel area. This will align your "power line" and provide a stiff jolt on contact.

The palm jab is very good as an initial shot, as it limits the opponent's vision or snaps the head back. It can be thrown with power or quickly thrown and attached to the face to set up a major blow or follow up.

THE REAR PALM THRUST – "HOU WOANG JERN"

This rear palm thrust is preformed with the hand turned with the fingers pointed outward. It is often used with lop sao and other H.I.A.'s. A rear vertical palm, "Yun Jern" is also frequently used. Like all rear attacks in Jun Fan, your hip and shoulder rote into the blow for maximum power.

SIDE VIEW

APPLICATION

THE PALM SLAP – "PAK JERN"

A palm slap is usually thrown to the side of the head to disorient an attacker. For maximum impact, relax your hand and swing your arm into the target with your elbow bent. Rotate your shoulder into the slap as you pivot in the ball of your lead foot. Slap through your target, not at it. For maximum impact. relax your hand and swing your arm into the target with your elbow bent. Rotate your shoulder into the slap as you pivot on the ball of your lead foot. Slap through your target, not at it. Spread your fingers slightly. Visualize your hand as a piece of clay. If you throw a piece of clay at any surface, it will mold into

FRONT VIEW

that surface upon impact. This will increase the shock and penetration of your slap.

FOLLOW THROUGH WHEN PRACTISING ON THE GLOVE

THE BACK FIST – "GUA CHUIE"

The back fist can be used at long range or trapping range. As with all Jun Fan hand strikes, the gua chuie should begin from the "on guard ready position" or applied during footwork. Throw your back fist straight to the point. Be sure not to cock your hand back, telegraphing your intention or you'll leave yourself open for a counter.

Instead of cocking your hand back, shift your hip and shoulder forward and transfer most of your weight to your front foot. Move your hand first, then shift forward as your hand explodes into your target. On contact, snap your wrist slightly forward as you clench your fist.

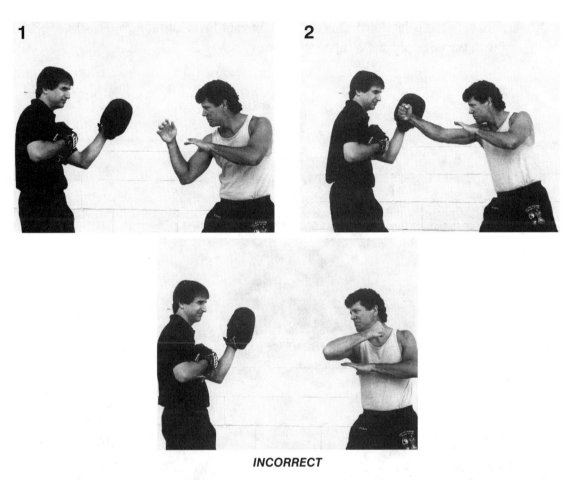

INCORRECT

APPLICATION

CHOPPING HAND – "SAUT SAO"

The saut sao is primarily a medium range hand technique, used frequently during a "hand immobilization attack" at trapping range. The mechanics of the saut sao are similar to the "gua chuie," but the hand shoots out in a hinge action, with the palm down. On contact snap your hand into the target, striking with the edge of hand or upper forearm.

FRONT VIEW

SIDE VIEW

APPLICATION

THE LEAD HOOK – "NAO CHUIE"

Although the lead hook is usually considered a short range power shot, it can actually be thrown at 3 ranges. Whichever range you throw your hook from, the principles of how you throw it will remain nearly the same. The hook can be used singly or as part of a compound attack, known as attack by combination or A.B.C.

To develop the basic mechanics of the hook shift your weight slightly back or to the opposite site of your body the hook is being thrown from. This is one body position used when throwing a hook. (When punching never shift 100 per

JUN FAN HOOK

TIGHT HOOK

JUN FAN HOOK

LOOSE HOOK

cent of your weight to one foot or the other.) As an example. if my weight is at 50-50, as I hook, I will shift my weight back about 75 per cent. My lead heel will raise slightly, pivoting on the ball of the foot. As I shift my hip and shoulder rotate into the blow. Notice the arm position and the fist, wrist and elbow alignment or "power line".

In most cases your arm is parallel to the ground, with exceptions of the shovel hook and overhand or down hook. The rear hand covers the other side of your head. Do not drop your rear hand, over rotate, or pull your hook into you. This leaves you open and makes your recovery slow. Your hand position can be horizontal, vertical, or quarter turned. All three are correct, find the one most comfortable for you personally. Don't bend at your wrist or you'll injure your wrist.

JUN FAN GUNG FU

APPLICATION

BODY HOOK

INCORRECT DELIVERY

INCORRECT DELIVERY

    The tight hook can be thrown to the body or the head or in combination. Keep your arm at a tight 90° angle. The power of your hook should follow the forearm line.

The loose hook is more relaxed and the forearm extends out from the 90° angle of the tight hook. Be sure not to wind up, pull back or lower your hand, avoid telegraphing. Always return to the guard position.

The long range "Jun Fan" lead hook is a blend of a loose hook and a straight punch. The major difference is you shift your body forward, pushing off with your rear foot. The angle of this modified hook is about 45°. Use shifting, explosive power when delivering this punch.

REAR HOOK – "HOU NAO GHUIE"

FRONT VIEW

The rear hook is a powerfully committed swing, best used as part of an A.B.C. As you rotate your hip. knee and shoulder into the blow while shifting your weight forward. Align the fist, wrist and elbow. Don't over rotate or reach for your target, this makes your recovery slow and easy to counter. It can be

SIDE VIEW

thrown as a tight or a loose hook. In any case always maintain your lead hand guard. Try not to wind up when you punch. Avoid telegraphing and always return to the guard position. A tight rear hook can be delivered to the head or the body. Keep your arm at about a 90° angle. The loose hook is more relaxed and the forearm is extended slightly. The rear hook can also be applied with lateral or triangular footwork. Step with your lead foot to add explosive power. as you shift into your punch.

THE SHOVEL HOOK

The shovel hook is a combination of a body hook and an uppercut. It can be done with the lead or rear hand and applied by shifting or with a step. The power is taken up from the ground by digging your toes into the floor. As you

FRONT VIEW

SIDE VIEW

APPLICATION

rotate, extend your leg, exploding into the target as you unload. An impressively powerful body shot, it's name comes from the shovel-like action.

THE UPPERCUT – "JIN CHUIE"

The uppercut is a close range weapon used for infighting. Generally in combination leading or following the tight hook. It's upward scooping motion is done with the palm facing you. The target can be the chin or the body. Keep a

RIGHT UPPERCUT

LEFT UPPERCUT

SIDE VIEW

strong, close guard protecting your jaw when in range for the uppercut, you're in tight hook range. Don't loop or drop your guard in preparation. Bend your knees slightly, and straighten them as you uppercut, shifting slightly up in to the target. Don't overshoot your target or throw the uppercut out of range or you will be easily countered.

APPLICATION

THE STRAIGHT BLAST – "JIK CHUNG CHUIE"

There are two types of straight blast punches. Short range "jik chung chuie" is an overwhelming barrage of straight battle punches. often used as a follow up after trapping or lin sil die da, the simultaneous parry and hit. When practicing

SEEKING THE PATH OF JEET KUNE DO

67

JUN FAN GUNG FU

this straight blast. start from the on guard position. As you extend your first punch. extend the last three knuckles in an upward direction into the target. As you retract that punch to your centerline, rotate your shoulder and snap out your second punch over the top of your retracting strike. This action is continued in a "rapid fire" set of elliptical motions. The target area for the "rapid fire" jik chung chuie is your opponent's centerline from his solar plexus to his nose. This straight blast method is borrowed from wing chun.

The second type of straight blast is a power blast. This is a slightly longer range variation developed by Sigung Bruce Lee and adapted to his personal

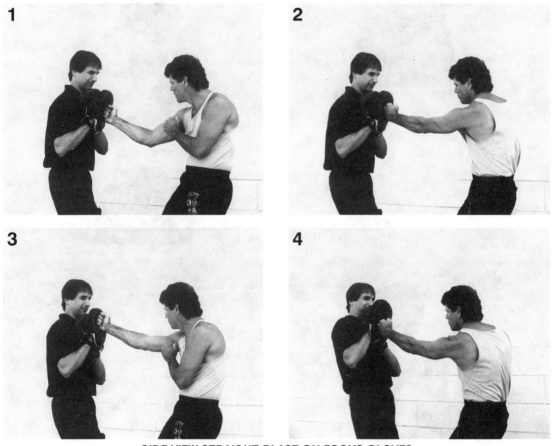

SIDE VIEW STRAIGHT BLAST ON FOCUS GLOVES

fighting method. To practice the "power blast" take a step with your lead foot and shift your weight forward into your lead straight. After your lead makes contact, retract it, while turning into your rear punch.

As you rotate your hip and shoulder, pivot your rear foot, digging it into the ground as you hit. The third punch is thrown by turning into your lead and exploding into your target. Be sure to maintain your "bai jong" prior to, and upon completion of the execution of your "power blast." Try to limit your "power blast" to 3, 4, or 5 punches in a set, otherwise it can become too energy-consuming, decreasing your power.

Be sure to have adequate padding to protect your partner when applying either "jik chung chuie" in practice. Always practice with safety in mind to avoid unnecessary injuries.

These are some of the basic hand techniques found in "Jun Fan". The technical form of your hand technique is very important. Following are some basic combinations to work on at the beginning level. The focus mitt should not be held loosely or rock solid, but with moderate resistance.

BASIC COMBINATIONS

1.) Double Jab

2.) Lead Jab, Rear Cross

3.) Lead Straight, Rear Cross

4.) Lead Finger Jab, Rear Cross

5.) Lead Jab, Rear Hook

6.) Rear Cross, Lead Hook

7.) Lead Jab, Rear Cross, Lead Hook

8.) Rear Cross, Lead Hook, Rear Cross

9. Lead Hook, Rear Cross. Lead Hook

10.) Lead Jab, Rear Cross, Lead Hook, Rear Cross

11.) Lead Jab, Rear Cross, Lead Uppercut

12. Lead Jab, Rear Uppercut, Lead Hook

13.) Lead Jab, Rear Cross, Lead Hook, Rear Uppercut

14.) Lead Jab, Lead Hook, Rear Uppercut, Lead Hook

OFFENSIVE HAND KEY POINTS TO REMEMBER

1. Be sure to review the section on offensive hand techniques regularly. This will give you a better overall picture and help solidify your mental image of the proper form. The more you visualize the proper form and constantly practice, the quicker you will improve.

2. Always be sure you are warmed up and well stretched before you begin. Proper warm-up and stretching promotes the elasticity of your muscles, prevents injuries and helps program your mind's state of readiness for training.

3. Always train with good form in mind. Don't sacrifice form for speed and power. As your form improves, your power will develop through proper body mechanics. With practice, your speed will improve. Strength plus speed equals power.

4. Try to isolate individual hand techniques and practice them on a regular basis. The combinations are very important. However, for the combinations to be strong, the individual tools must be structurally correct. Tool isolation and development is an important concept of Jeet Kune Do. Regardless of their skill level, pro boxers still practice their jab every workout. Pro basketball players still practice freethrows every practice session, and pro baseball players will always have batting practice. Remember, "repetition is the mother of skill."

SIFU FRANCIS FONG OF ATLANTA, GEORGIA DEMONSTRATING FINER POINTS OF HAND TECHNIQUES

QUESTIONS ABOUT OFFENSIVE HAND TECHNIQUES

Q. As a Karate student I was taught that power was generated by rotation of your torso by pulling your opposite shoulder back as you thrust forward. How do you get any power with the JKD punching method?

A. The way power is generated in karate, is just a different way of approaching the art of striking. One similarity is, in both arts power is brought up from the ground. The power in Jun Fan Gung Fu is brought up from the ground by pushing away from the ground and projecting forward as you torque into the blow. By synchronising the motion with your body alignment, you increase the power. The order of initiation should be hand, shoulder, hip, foot pushing off as you torque into the blow.

Q. Do I have to wear gloves when I hit the heavy bag? My friend told me he doesn't really think it matters.

A. Absolutely it matters, you should wear bag gloves with a solid enough foam padding over the knuckle. If you hit the heavy bag hard, you should wrap your hands with gauze or boxing hand wraps. I prefer elastic Mexican style hand wraps and a boxing glove style bag glove. Not protecting your hands can cause joint problems.

Q. What's more powerful, a punch or a palm strike?

A. I believe a palm strike is more powerful when striking the head. The palm strike is concave and the head is convex. If the palm is used in a relaxed and heavy fashion like a slap a tremendous amount of power can be generated thru the target. Punches will however have greater penetration to the body. Another point to consider is that on the street punching the head can be risky as you could break your hand or cut your hand on teeth risking disease or infection. It is my opinion that at times open hand strikes may be more appropriate for the head and punches more effective for the body.

"When I first started training with Sifu Bruce, he was in the midst of creating a "system" of combat that centered around a modified form of Wing Chun, a blending of his modifications and ideas on the strategies of Western boxing, and then using the principles and tactics for Western fencing. He took kicking from different systems, including Chinese and non-Chinese systems, then customized it for himself. He was into investigating every known system that he was exposed to during that time period."
– Sifu Dan Inosanto

LESSON 4
BASIC FOCUS GLOVE FEED DRILLS

In this chapter in addition to the application offensive hand techniques I'd like to introduce you to some basic feed drills found in Western boxing and some intermediate focus glove drills from Jun Fan Gung Fu. I will also introduce you to a basic catch and return drill. This is a good supplementary drill to focus glove training and is found in more detail in volume two of my video.

The first is one of many focus glove drills where the partner or coach dictates or controls the action. It is important to practice the basics often to develop good form and a relaxed, responsive flow during practice.

In ring fight training the fighter will maintain a specific lead during focus glove or mitt training. For the Jun Fan student however the drill should be done from both leads. The holder has fundamental two jobs, to hold the "mitt" for the puncher and to feed specific offensive motions to develop specific reactions.

The holder is now the coach and dictates the pace of the round as well as the intensity. The holder, in the role of coach must guide the puncher verbally as to the areas that require more work or improvement. As you hold, be that person's eyes and look for the openings in their defense, their punching form, application of footwork, correct range, proper focus, breathing etc.

As you progress you will naturally pick up the qualities of speed, power, timing and focus, don't rush these areas until your form is correct. As you develop your form your other attributes will also develop.

Once you have a level of competency with your focus glove boxing, integrate the kicking into your rounds as well. We will discuss many levels of focus glove training in my next book.

THE BASIC HOLDS

Start in a matched stance. To signal you to right jab, your partner flashes the right mitt. To signal a cross flash the opposite mitt. A jab, cross, hook is signaled by holding the mitt at a right angle. If the holder says, "one, two," a jab, cross, hook, cross is thrown. If the holder holds the right or left mitt at a low (abdominal height) position, this signals a body hook to be thrown. A right or left uppercut is held at a 45 degree angle facing your partner.

JAB POSITION

CROSS POSITION

HOLD THE MITT AT 90° ANGLE FOR THE HOOK

BODY HOOK POSITION

UPPERCUT POSITION

THE BASIC FEEDS

At this point we'll be introduced to three basic feeds. The first feed will resemble a jab. Your partner has two reasons for this feed. The first is to be sure that your jab returns to the correct position. This is done with the flat of the glove. The second reason is to get a "catch and jab" counter response. Be sure not to hold the rear mitt in front of your face as you feed.

The second feed is in the form of a rear cross or rear hook to your head. Be sure to practice and review the section on the bob and weave paying strict attention to your form. As your partner feeds, bob and weave to the outside of the blow and return a lead hook/rear cross counter. Take your time, being aware of body mechanics as you follow up. The third feed is fed as a lead hook to the side of your head. As you read the attack, bob and weave into the direction of the blow. After dipping under the hook, your body should be torqued in preparation of unleashing a rear cross/lead hook combination immediately after the evasion.

Chain all the holds and feeds together, and eventually add the basic combinations listed, mixing the sequence arbitrarily as you continue. Start slow, paying attention to details in form, balance and body mechanics. Start with two, three-minute rounds of continuous movement with a one minute rest between rounds and build from there. As you and your partner improve, add the holds for the combinations shown at the end of lesson 3 to this drill to increase the degree of difficulty.

Following are a few of the intermediate focus glove drills taught to me by Sifu Dan Inosanto.

SWING THE REAR HOOK OR CROSS TO PROMPT A BOB AND WEAVE REACTION

WHEN YOU FEED THE LEAD HOOK YOUR PARTNER SHOULD BOB AND WEAVE IN THE OPPOSITE DIRECTION

FOCUS GLOVE DRILLS
INTERMEDIATE FEEDS
1-2 (JAB-CROSS) COUNTER SERIES

1. Catch & Shoulder Roll a. W/ Low Round Kick (Nao Tek) b. W/ Low Side Kick (Juk Tek)
   c. W/ Low Snap Kick (1 Tek)
   Add Cross/Hook/Cross/2 Kicks
2. Catch & Bob & Weave
   Add Hook/Cross/Hook/2 Kicks
3. Catch & Insert
   a. Shoulder Stop b. Bicep Stop c. Straight Arm Deflection d. Bent Arm Deflection (Bil Sao)
   Add Cross/Hook/Cross/2 Kicks
4. Catch & Inside Deflection
   a. Return High Cross/Hook/Cross b. Return Low Cross/Hook/Cross
   Add Any 2 Kicks

1-3 (LEAD JAB-LEAD HOOK) COUNTER SERIES

1. Catch & Bob & Weave Add Cross/Hook/Cross/2 Kicks
2. Catch & Head Cover
   Add Hook/Cross/Hook/2 Kicks
3. Catch & Cover & Hit
   a. Cover & Hit b. Bent Arm Deflection & Hit (Bil Da) c. Vertical Palm Block (Jong Da) d. Palm Up Block (Tan Da)
   Add Cross/Hook/Cross/2 Kicks
4. Catch & Pivot/Shoulder Stop
   Add Cross/Hook/Cross/2 Kicks
5. Catch & Step ThruW/Shoulder Stop
   Add Simultaneous Knee/Cross/Hook/Cross/2 Kicks

BASIC CATCH AND RETURN DRILL

This drill is a very good way to integrate some of your hand techniques with active footwork. Catch drills help the student develop good judgment, correct timing and body mechanics in a controlled environment. They're also excellent for improving your balance and agility when moving. In the beginning drill (single riposte) we're going to limit the feed to a lead jab only. We'll also limit your response to five basics. Be sure to wear some type of hand protection such as padded bag gloves. These offer a margin of safety for both of you.

The first basic response we're going to cover is the catch. The concept behind the catch is to time the opponent's jab and replace the intended target with

DURING THE FLOW OF THE ROUND FEED YOUR PARTNER SHOULD JAB WHILE HOLDING THE OTHER FOCUS GLOVE AS A TARGET

your rear hand. To effectively apply the catch, you must control the distance, so your partner has to step in to land his lead attack. As his commitment is made, sway back to maintain the margin of distance. When his lead jab is at full extension, return your lead jab. If your partner steps deep, step and slide back as you sway.

The catch can also be applied by patting down the jab before you return. The third basic is rear pak sao and return. Be sure to clear the path before returning your jab. The fourth basic is rear pak and low return. To help to ensure your success, this should be done simultaneously. The fifth basic is rear tan sao and return. To aid in your success here, step or slip right as you tan da. The timing on your return can be immediately after your catch or parry.

However, always be aware of the possibility of the rear hand following. Work the catch drill slowly and rhythmically, at first with one person feeding. Keep moving and vary the timing, working both leads as you improve. Be sure to practice maintaining the correct form of each technique in the combination. Bring your hand back to your jaw each time, after you throw each punch.

CHAPTER CONCLUSION

These are examples of the above drills on a basic level. Remember to start slow, but continuous as you feed your partner. What we want to achieve on the foundational level is the ability to read the action, react, and flow continuously. As you improve, pick up the pace and feed other single direct attacks or attack by combinations (see Chapter 5 to review some of the defensive hand techniques necessary for the catch and return drill). As the feeder, you not only provide the action and the targets for reaction, but you are also developing your role as a coach. Pay close attention to your partner's technical form. In the beginning stages of your development, body mechanics and structural form are far more important than speed and power.

I prefer to teach by principles, concepts and strategies, because they seem to go beyond the confines and boundaries of any one particular system or style.
Truth is not limited by national boundaries. Truth is derived from self-discovery. If you truly seek it with your heart and soul, whether it is in the martial arts or any other area of your life, you will find it.
– Sifu Dan Inosanto

LESSON 5
DEFENSIVE HAND TECHNIQUES

Although, ultimately the goal in Jun Fan is to counter hit, stop hit or parry and hit, whenever possible. In order to be able to accomplish these you must be proficient in your technical defensive application, timing and footwork. Your need for basic blocks and parries are very important factors in the success of your defense.

To understand the basis of Jun Fan's four corner defense, we'll look at it from the application of various attacks. This helps us set the groundwork for learning the purpose of each of the defensive tools used in Jun Fan. The upper body is broken up into four gates or zones which an opponent will attack. For the sake of simplicity, we will number each gate from 1 thru 4. The inside leg and outside leg are gates 5 and 6, and are defended by shielding with your legs, countering by stop kicking the attacker's legs, head or body, or using evasive footwork.

The inside perimeter of each gate runs down the center is called the centerline. The outside perimeter of each gate is just past your shoulder. A horizontal line designates each area as high and low. The high horizontal perimeter is just above the forehead and the low horizontal perimeter is at mid thigh. There is also a lead and rear dimension.

As you begin practicing your defensive hand techniques, isolate each block individually while practicing. Later, as you develop precision in the timing and execution of your defense your parries will be applied with a counter or simultaneous attack whenever possible.

Blocks and parries require a good deal of practice and can be very abusive on your partner. Some of the blocks are designed to penetrate the muscle or dis-

JUN FAN GUNG FU

rupt the nerve flow. Be aware of your level of control and your partner will be appreciative.

**FRONT VIEW
(WEIGHT FORWARD BAI JONG)**

SIDE VIEW

**FRONT VIEW
(WEIGHT BACK)**

SLAPPING HAND – "PAK SAO"

The pak sao is used at long range, mid range and trapping range and is a key component in Jun Fan trapping. It can be used to parry an attack to any of the 4 gates. The lead and rear pak sao can be done either high or low. The high lead pak sao is used to guard gate 1 and the low lead pak sao gate 3, while the rear pak sao can be used to guard gates 2 and 4.

LEAD PAK SAO

REAR PAK SAO

REAR LOW PAK SAO

To apply your pak sao correctly your hand should be relaxed and heavy, not stiff upon contact. This will increase the penetration of your pak sao and allow you to stick to your opponent's arm when necessary. The high lead pak sao is used to guard gate 1. The rear pak sao can be used to guard gate 2.

LEAD PAK SAO THE JAB

REAR PAK SAO THE JAB

PALM UP BLOCK – "TAN SAO"

Tan sao can be used to cut or deflect a straight line attack to either gate 1 or gate 2 or draw his energy past you using "Lie Sao", a palm-up pulling hand version of tan sao. Rear tan sao is used by shifting or stepping to the outside line of gate 2 and is usually applied with a strike or "Tan Da".

The tan sao in Jun Fan can be done with the wrist straight or bent depending on the application. However the guarding center tan sao wrist is always straight and the energy must shoot forward. "Guarding Center Tan Sao" is often used to defend against a compound hand immobilization attack or H.I.A.

LEAD TAN SAO

LEAD TAN SAO THE LEAD PUNCH

LIE SAO DA TO DEFEND THE REAR CROSS

REAR TAN DA

USING TAN SAO TO DEFEND PAK SAO DA

LOW OUTSIDE CUT – "GOANG SAO"

Goang sao can be described as a low outside cutting arm block. It is very powerful, but should be done relaxed and firm, not stiff. Goang sao can be used to cut or deflect a straight line or curved line attack. As an opponent strikes to your 4th gate, sweep your hand down and outward. Keep your elbow slightly bent cutting through the attack in a relaxed slicing motion. "Woang Ha Pak", a low outside slapping parry, or "Kao Sao", a scooping block, can also be used.

Rear goang sao is used to cut or deflect an attack to gate 3 with a slice parallel to the mid section. When a strike is done with a goang sao, it is called "Goang Da".

JUN FAN GUNG FU

LEAD GO ANG SAO

CUTTING THE OPPONENTS LOW JAB WITH A GO ANG SAO

USING GO ANG SAO TO SHIELD A LOW BODY HOOK

THRUSTING FORWARD BLOCK – "BIL SAO"

Bil sao can guard against a straight or curved line attack to gate 1 or 2. It can also be used to gain an attachment or reference point for trapping and grabbing during an H.I.A. Bil sao can also be done in a palm down position or with the wrist slightly turned.

One thing that characterizes bil sao from most blocks is its thrusting energy. Combined with a strong structural form, bil sao is effective against most curved line attacks. When bil sao is used against a curved line attack the hand's position should be at a 45° and the forearm at a diagonal both upward and outward. The bicep line should be almost horizontal.

When "Bil Da" is used to counter a curved line attack, it is applied with a straight line attack cutting the opponent's energy and attacking his centerline.

LEAD BIL SAO

DEFLECTING A LEAD STRAIGHT

BIL SAO CAN EASILY TRANSFORM INTO BIL GEE

JUN FAN GUNG FU

LEAD BIL SAO USED TO COUNTER A REAR HOOK

USING REAR BIL SAO DA TO DIFUSE A LEAD HOOK TO HEAD

LOW CENTER BRIDGE – "CHUNG JIOANG"

The "Chung Jioang" is similar to Wing Chun's "Jut Sao". The lead center block is used to guard gate 3. against an attack too powerful for "Ha Pak" such as a body hook or thrust kick, by dropping your forearm into the attack. To perform the chung jioang correctly your forearm should be at a 45°, yet not quite horizontal. Your elbow should be lower than your hand and your elbow about a distance of one fist away from your body. If any of the three components is missing, your structure will be off and you'll get hit.

LEAD CHUNG JIOANG

LEAD CENTRE BLOCK TO COUNTER A REAR HOOK...

OR A LEAD HOOK

WING ARM DEFLECTION – "BONG SAO"

The bong sao is a deflecting technique mostly used at mid-range and in trapping. Its main function is to roll upward and/or inward, creating a plane for deflecting and dissolving the energy of an opponent's straight line attack past the intended target. Bong sao can be done high or low. It can also be modified in the high position to bridge the forward energy of an attack. Bong sao will become an integral part, as we become more involved in simple and compound trapping later in this book and future volumes.

JUN FAN GUNG FU

LEAD BONG SAO

LEAD BONG SAO USED TO DEFLECT A REAR STRAIGHT PUNCH

OUTSIDE GRABBING HAND – "LOP SAO"

Lop sao is a combination of grabbing and pulling. It can be applied with the lead or rear hand, anytime there is contact with your opponent's arm to the outside of your wrist or forearm. As your opponent punches; block, bridging into the attack to gain an attachment. This can be done using tan sao, bil sao, or bong sao. As you grab, pull the punch to your hip while shifting your weight

to your rear leg. Be sure your rear heel is flat on the ground and your hip bone line up with your rear foot on a vertical plane. As you pull your opponent in, drop your weight slightly as you shoot out your counter. The power of your strike will be compounded by the pulling energy, as your palm or fist meets the target. If you block with one hand and lop with the other, it's referred to as cross grab or "lin lop sao." If you pass the punch by deflecting it to the lopping hand, I call it a "passover."

SEEKING THE PATH OF JEET KUNE DO

BONG SAO TO LIN LOP SAO TO SUT SAO HIT

BONG SAO TO LOP SAO TO WOANG JERN HIT

LOP SAO TO LOP SAO DRILL

This is a very good basic energy drill. For the purposes of learning; in the beginning; stand facing your partner. Later your stance can be adjusted. As your partner punches lop sao with your same hand. After you lop, return the punch with that hand. When you punch, your partner will lop sao your punching hand. This completes one cycle of the drill. To switch hands in the beginning stage of this drill pin the hand being pulled by pushing it into your partner. As the arm is pushed, your partner rotates and lin lop sao's the pushing hand, and the cycle continues. This drill will greatly improve your ability to sink your weight and help develop your balance and sensitivity.

Although many of the blocks, parries and defensive principles found in "Jun Fan" come from Wing Chun gung fu, they have in most cases been modified and applied to the Jun Fan structure. However Wing Chun is considered one of the "core arts" of Jun Fan.

In order to develop the fundamentals necessary for a strong foundation in Jun Fan and Jeet Kune Do, it is essential that you continue to practice the material on defensive hand techniques on a regular basis.

SEEKING THE PATH OF JEET KUNE DO

1) PARTNER DOES A RIGHT PUNCH – BONG WITH YOUR RIGHT ARM 2) LOP SAO WITH THE SAME HAND THEN PUNCH IMMEDIATELY 3) YOUR PARTNER THEN LOPS. 4) AS YOUR PARTNER PUNCHES AGAIN YOU LOP SAO. 5) TO SWITCH HANDS USE GUM SAO PINNING HIS ARM FORCING HIM TO CROSS GRAB THE PUSHING HAND.

DEFENSIVE HAND KEY POINTS TO REMEMBER

1.) Practice your defensive hand techniques with good form in mind. Always start out slow and use caution.
2.) Develop your parries and blocks singularly before applying them against "compound attacks". Once you feel confident when blocking an attack use them to defend against a multiple attack.
3.) Although many of the blocks found in Jun Fan come from Wing Chun Gung Fu, they have, in most cases, been modified and applied to a different structure. However, Wing Chun is considered the "core art" of Jun Fan.
4). Remember, what you are learning are basics.

You Have often heard people quote Sifu Bruce Lee as saying, "Jeet Kune Do is not the accumulation of knowledge, but the hacking away at the unessential." But do they truly understand what they preach? For the accumulation of knowledge and hacking away at the unessential is not a product, but a process. It is a continual process that lasts our entire lives. We are constantly accumulating and eliminating, then again accumulating and eliminating.
– Sifu Dan Inosanto

LESSON 6
SIMULTANEOUS BLOCK & STRIKE – "LIN SIL DIE DA"

"Lin Sil Die Da", though very simple in concept and theory, is very difficult to implement in practice. It requires a skilled level of timing and can only be mastered after much practice.

A major concept of the Wing Chun system, Lin Sil Die Da is derived on the premise of stop hitting by blocking or parrying, and hitting simultaneously. This is also known as a single time hit counter. One of the main characteristics of single time hits is they must be straight to the point, utilizing the shortest distance between your tool and the target area. Sliding energy or cutting the tool (the opponent's arm) as you thrust toward your destination may be necessary to deflect the incoming strike in some cases.

An excellent way to practice is with a boxing glove on the lead hand and a focus mitt on the rear hand for a target. Have your partner feed the lead punch to each of the four gates one at a time so isolate each technique. Do not hold the focus glove in front of your face, instead use it to catch the counter. Use care and control until your accuracy is assured.

SINGLE TIME HIT COUNTERS

In this section we'll cover the application of single time hits to your four corner defense with a partner. We're going to separate this into two methods.

a. Lead block or parry and rear strike – the most powerful, though least efficient.

b. Rear block or parry and lead strike – the most efficient and economical of the two methods.

Let's begin with the lead block/rear strike.

LEAD BLOCK REAR STRIKE

As your opponent attacks gate one, respond with a lead pak sao and a rear straight line attack. Sigung Lee preferred using the finger jab. However for the purpose of safety, we suggest using the straight punch when practicing with your partner. Always use caution and control while practicing. When your pak sao parries past your strike. it's referred to as "woang pak."

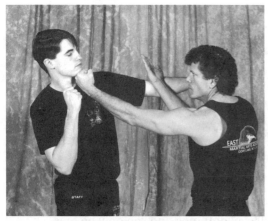

AGAINST A REAR STRAIGHT

AGAINST A LEAD JAB

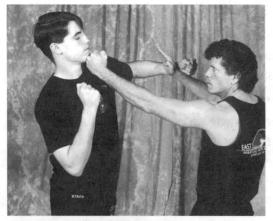

AGAINST A HOOK

AGAINST A CROSS

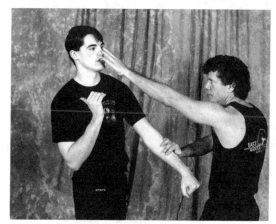

AGAINST A BODY PUNCH

AGAINST A BODY PUNCH

As my opponent leads with his right, I counter with "loy woang pak da." If my opponent attempts a rear cross, he's countered by "noy woang pak da." From an unmatched stance, such as left to right the opposite would be true. If attacked in gate two, I counter with "noy tan da" or "loy tan da." If a rear hook is thrown turn your hand over into bil sao da. When an attack enters gate three, "ha pak da," or "doan da" is applied. To defend gate four, "woang ha pak da," a low outside parry or "goang da," the low outside cutting block.

REAR BLOCK/LEAD STRIKE

The most efficient method of block and hit focuses on JKD's principle of utilizing the closest tool, nearest to the target. As your partner leads with a jab or a rear cross to gate one, apply a rear tan/lead hit counter. Take a short step and shift to the right to increase efficiency and safety. Always be aware of the possibility of the rear cross following the lead jab. If the lead hook is thrown, continue the rotation of your forearm into the bil sao position. Your timing is imperative, if you don't react immediately with your counter, you could get hit by the rear hand.

AGAINST A LEAD STRAIGHT

AGAINST A JAB

The next attack is to gate two. You have three basic options off of this attack. The first is "woang pak noy da," simultaneous block and hit to the outside line. The second option is "woang pak ha da," high parry, low hit. The third is "noy pak loy da," an outside parry inside hit, also known as a split entry. The next attack we'll address is to gate three. Gate three is defended using "woang ha pak da," low outside parry or "goang da," low outside cutting block. The final area is gate four. As the straight line attack enters gate four, apply "ha pak da." Be sure to return your lead hand to the guard position, in case his rear hand follows his low lead. A simultaneous block and hit is classified as a single time hit. A time hit is a stop hit timed to land while simultaneously preventing the opponent attack. Even though these time hits are simple in context they require precise timing and body mechanics, and constant practice, in order to make them work.

AGAINST A CROSS

AGAINST A LEAD JAB

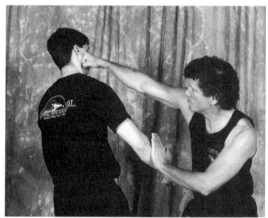
AGAINST A BODY PUNCH

AGAINST A BODY PUNCH

DOUBLE TIME HIT COUNTERS

Another time hit I'd like to cover in this section is called a double time counter. In a double time counter, you parry and hit with the same hand. Here are just a couple of examples. As your partner feeds you a right jab, parry with your lead and return a lead straight punch or back fist. Use your rear hand to monitor his punch after you parry, you can then use it for a quick follow up. If your partner feeds you a left jab from an unmatched lead, use the exact same method. A double time hit can also be used against a low jab. thrown from a right or a left lead.

JUN FAN GUNG FU

PAK INSIDE WITH YOUR LEAD – THEN HIT WITH YOUR LEAD STRIKE WHILE MONITORING HIS ATTACK WITH YOUR REAR HAND.

PARRY PARTNERS CROSS WITH A LEAD PAK – FOLLOW UP WITH A LEAD STRIKE.

APPLYING TIMING TO SPARRING

The use of timing is fundamental to the JKD fighter. By using your tools at the right moment you optimize their value. In Jeet Kune Do, the Why, Where and How to is important. But to be successful "When" is the key.

What is Rhythm? Rhythm is measured sound or movement with a consistent or uniform recurrence of a beat. In all motion one can find an established rhythm. As you will notice each individual has a natural rhythm when they move. While training try to identify your personal rhythm. While training drills with a partner or during light sparring be aware of their rhythm. Once you are aware of these rhythms then you can work on breaking your rhythm during light sparring. You can suddenly break your rhythm between you and your opponent by stalling, feinting, slight hesitation, or varying the speed of your rhythm and hitting your opponent on the half beat. Hitting on the half beat is a counter strike that is executed just before your opponent can hit or in between any two attacks during the rhythm of their attacking sequence. The half beat can be applied for example just before they jab. A one and a half beat

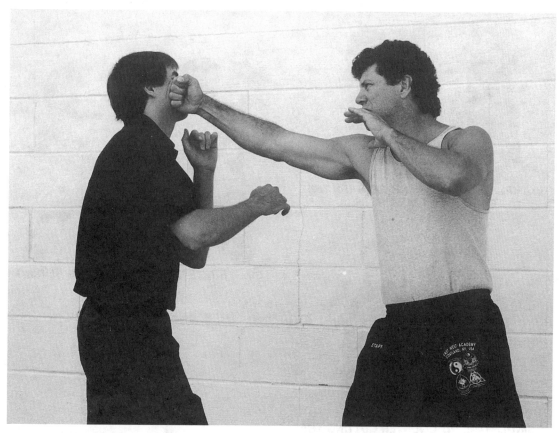

HITTING ON THE HALF BEAT – JUST BEFORE THE OPPONENT ATTACKS

applied in between their jab – cross, (sneak in your fast jab just before they cross) or maybe cross between the cross hook of their jab-cross-hook combination (2 ½ beat). Broken rhythm is an invaluable tool for improving your sparring or competitive fighting.

"Sifu Bruce Lee practiced what he preached, living by his own creed:
1. "Jeet Kune Do utilizes all ways and is bound by none."
2. "Jeet Kune Do is finding the cause of your own ignorance."
3. "Using No Way as Way" and "Having no limitation as limitation."
4. "Absorb what is useful, reject what is useless and add what is specifically your own."

It is important that a student in Jeet Kune Do have a good foundation in the Jun Fan method of Gung Fu before he expands, explores and "Absorbs What Is Useful" for his own personal system of Jeet Kune Do."

Dan Inosanto

EXAMPLE OF 1½ CROSSING BETWEEN THE OPPONENT'S JAB/CROSS

SINGLE TIME HIT COUNTER USING SLIDING ENERGY

A SINGLE TIME HIT COUNTER CUTTING THE OPPONENT'S TOOL

QUESTIONS ABOUT
LIN SIL DIE DA

Q. Hitting to counter my opponent as he hits seems difficult. How can I improve my skills at this?

A. This skill is difficult. To improve your skill, chunk down three different single time counters for one specific attack and isolate each one 15-20 times with your partner, then chain each one by adding separately until you have all three in any order. Practice the three basics you have chosen until they feel natural and can be done responsively when your partner punches. Expand the formula and practice using the catch and return drill format in Chapter 4. As you improve, apply when sparring.

Q. Do any other martial arts other than Jun Fan block and hit simultaneously?

A. Yes, actually most martial arts do so in the advanced training. Jun Fan adapted it's single time counters (simultaneous block and hit counters) from Wing Chun Gung Fu and western boxing. Both arts, though very different apply this idea very effectively.

Q. When I try to hit simultaneously sometimes I get clipped by my buddy's punch. Why am I getting hit?

A. It's hard for me to tell for sure without seeing what you're doing, but more than likely it's your angle or your timing. You can gain an edge of security by emphasizing the angle at which you are hitting by putting your shoulder behind your punch or tilting your head slightly out of the trajectory of the incoming blow. Another problem that may occur is in your timing. When your timing is late the initiator has the power line and they will cut your energy, deflecting your strike.

Each student must depart on his own journey to find what is workable for them in philosophy, technique, tactics, strategies and principles in the Jun Fan method and then explore other methods that interest them.
Sifu Dan Inosanto

LESSON 7
BASIC KICKING TECHNIQUES

Most Jun Fan kicking techniques are done below the horizontal perimeter of gates 1 and 2. Low and mid line kicking has many advantages. The target is closer, you require less time, your balance is not as compromised, and these kicks, especially leg kicks are more difficult to defend against.

In most cases kicks in Jun Fan are not chambered. Bruce Lee felt that chambering a kick did not increase its power and would telegraph your intention, therefore making it less effective. Practice your kicks using different targets. The feel of a heavy bag is different than kicking a shield, or a pair of focus mitts or Thai pads.

To become well rounded you should also practice in the air isolating each kick, by shadow boxing, and with a partner defending your kick.

Always be sure your legs are warmed up and well stretched before you attempt any kicks with power. Be sure not to extend your knee joint all the way when you kick, this can result in injury due to hyperextension. Never kick violently or with intensity in the air to keep your legs strong and injury free. If you want to kick hard, kick the heavy bag, shield or Thai pads. Also be aware of the floor surface, if abrasive it could prevent you from pivoting your foot properly causing an ankle or knee injury.

Kicking also has two major advantages over hand techniques. First, you can attack or counter from a greater distance. Second, your legs can physiologically supply you with more power than your hands. A good kicking repertoire makes it harder for your opponent to close the distance and reach you with his hands.

Kicking is also a very effective way to close the distance and set up hand combinations. To increase your strength and power, work the drills in Chapter 2, to improve your overall kicking, in the words of Bruce Lee "kick".

LEAD SNAP KICK – "JIN TEK"

Initially all kicks should be practiced without stepping but by shifting your weight back. Later we will expand on various ways to apply your kicks with footwork.

The main target for the snap kick is the groin. The kick should progress vertically to the target by lifting your knee and snapping your lower leg in a rising hinge motion. Sometimes referred to as the uppercut kick, the striking surface is the instep or shin depending upon distance. Relax as you kick and recover fully to a completely balanced and ready position.

REAR SNAP KICK – "HOU JIN TEK"

The basic mechanics are the same as the lead but you swing your leg forward in a straight line snapping it into your target. You can retract your kick to stay out of punching range or step down to close the distance. If you follow up with your lead hand, be sure you hit before you step down. This projects the power of your punch into the target, not the ground.

LEAD FRONT KICK – "JIK LEK"

The "Jik Tek" is used in a similar way to the lead jab, and is sometimes referred to as the foot jab. It makes an exceptional stop-kick, to stop an opponent from closing the gap to punching range. To apply a front kick lift your knee as your foot begins to move forward and thrust out your kick all in one motion. Contact is made with the ball of the foot. On contact lean back slightly and thrust your hip forward, through your target. This should be done as you complete your thrust, for maximum power.

  As you lift your foot tilt your hips back slightly. Bring your knee up and into the target while snapping out your lower leg and rotating your hip into the subject. Target areas include the thigh, inner thigh, at the hip, solar plexus, ribs, and on rare openings, the head.

JUN FAN GUNG FU

REAR FRONT KICK – "HOU JIK TEK"

To apply the rear jik tek, step through as you lift your knee and thrust your kick out. Rotate your hip into the target and on contact lean back, thrusting your hip forward focusing through your . subject, as you complete your thrust. Contact is made with the ball of the foot. The leg can be retracted or you can step in with a follow up.

SEEKING THE PATH OF JEET KUNE DO

109

LEAD STOMP KICK – "DUM TEK"

The mechanics of the stomp kick are similar to the the foot jab. but the whole bottom of the foot is used. The front foot jab is fast, penetrating kick. The strength of the stomp kick is found in its powerful blast, easily able to kick down a door or stop a charging opponent in their tracks knocking them to the ground.

REAR STOMP KICK – "HOU DUM TEK"

The rear stomp is one of the most powerful kicks in the Jun Fan kicking arsenal. Although very committed once it is begun, it will literally launch most partners across the room when impact is made with the kicking shield of even the most prepared holder. As with the lead stomp make contact with your target using the whole bottom of your foot as the striking tool. Remember to project your energy through the target while staying as balanced and controlled as possible. A prepared, strong and ready recovery is important when applying any kick

SEEKING THE PATH OF JEET KUNE DO

LEAD SIDE KICK – "JUK TEK"

The lead side kick is a key component of the Jun Fan "Jeet Tek" or stop kick. It is generally used to attack the opponents lead leg or mid section. It's also an excellent way to close the distance or "Chum Kil" into punching or trapping range. It can be applied as a side thrust, a snap or held out straight as a lead leg obstruction to jam your opponents advance or lead kick. When applying this kick don't chamber your kick, let it fly from the ground directly to the target like a magnet to an iron surface.

JUN FAN GUNG FU

截拳道

LEAD SIDE KICK

MID SIDE KICK

LOW STOP KICK

PRACTICE ON SHIELD FOR POWER

REAR SIDE KICK – "HOU JUK TEK"

The rear side kick is powerful, but easily detectable due to it's lack of directness. Because it is slower, it is usually used as a low leg attack, or to the body of a slower opponent. As you step through, rotate your hip, while thrusting out your kick. Use the whole bottom of your foot when side kicking.

LEAD HOOK KICK OR ROUND KICK – "NAO TEK'

The lead round kick or hook kick as Bruce Lee used to refer to it, is one of the fastest, non-telegraphic kicks in Jun Fan Gung Fu. It lacks the power of the lead side kick, but is very effective when used correctly. When applied with advancing footwork the power can be increased dramatically.

As you begin your lead nao tek lift your foot as you tilt your hips back slightly. As you do this bring your knee up and into the target while quickly snapping out your lower leg and rotating your hips into the subject. The striking surface you will use to attack with is the lower shin and instep. Your target areas are the calf, inner thigh, groin, rib and on rare openings the head.

JUN FAN GUNG FU

LOW ROUND KICK

PRACTICE ON FOCUS GLOVES FOR ACCURACY AND IMPACT

MID LEVEL STOP ROUND KICK

REAR ROUND KICK – "HOU NAO TEK"

The rear round kick is very powerful. It is best used as part of an attack by combination. Because of its total commitment, it goes through the target with explosive force. When using your rear round kick, swing the hip, leg, and shoulder into the target, while pivoting on the ball of your lead foot and pushing off

EXPLOSIVE POWER CAN ONLY BE EXPERIENCED BY TRAINING ON THE KICKSHIELD

with your rear foot. Keep your knee bent on contact. The striking areas are the mid to lower shin and instep. The chief targets of the rear round kick are the calf thigh, and midsection. It can be used as a follow up to the head with knock out power. To cut your opponent's defensive line and add power use a triangle step into the target.

LEAD SCOOP KICK

The lead scoop kick could be described as a lifting instep strike. This strike is used at close range, usually after shin to shin engagement during trapping. The lifting motion slides up the leg in a scooping action. The target area is the groin, a primary target in Jun Fan.

FRONT VIEW

SIDE VIEW

APPLICATION

INVERTED HOOK KICK – "LOY TEK"

This kick is used as a lead leg attack to the groin, inside thigh or side of the knee. Applied to an opponent in an unmatched stance, the foot and shin are angled inward to penetrate the defense. The power is generated opening the hip, while lifting and snapping out the leg.

SEEKING THE PATH OF JEET KUNE DO

PRACTICE ON FOCUS GLOVES FOR TARGET

TOE SNAP KICK – "JIT TEK"

Sometimes called a nail kick, the jit tek is a snap kick using the toe of your shoe. Target areas include the groin, the legs, kidney area, the solar plexus, and upon rare opportunity, the throat and head.

TARGET AND IMPACT PRACTICE ON SHIELD

OBLIQUE KICK – "HOU DUM TEK"

The oblique can be performed as a low cross stomp "dum tek" or in a sweeping straight trajectory "pak tek". It can be applied as a short distracting entrance, in combination or as a stop kick. Bear in mind that a stop kick can be used to stop an opponent while they are attacking, or to physically stop the attacking weapon itself. A foot stomp is probably the most effective close quarter kick. It is extremely powerful, having the ground to support the target from below. It is easily capable of breaking the foot, and it is very difficult to detect or block. By breaking the opponent's foot, you make it difficult for him to continue his attack, pursue you, or escape.

OBLIQUE STOP-KICK

APPLICATION

PRACTICE THE OBLIQUE KICK ON SHIELD

BACK KICK – "HOU TEK"

The back kick is a very powerful mid to long range attack similar to the side kick. The difference is, with the back kick you rotate your hip turning your back to the target. Your knee and foot will point down diagonally as you thrust out your kick. Your heel will provide the striking surface. The back kick can be used to give you a slight extension to your side kick, to reach a retreating opponent, defend against an attack from behind, or as a quick follow up after your kick has been parried. Sigung Bruce used this powerful kick, at times with a step behind shuffle, blasting a sometimes unsuspecting holder backwards with incredible impact.

PRACTICE BACK KICK ON THE SHIELD

FOUR DISTANCES OF LEAD KICKS

1.) Stationary Kick
To apply this kick, visualize flicking water off of your foot without any step or preparation.

2.a.) Pendulum Kick
A pendulum kick is used to apply various lead kicks quickly closing the distance. Sort of an abbreviated version of the standard shuffle, it also gives you the capability of moving in and out using your kick to probe.

2.b.) Push Step Kick
This is the same distance as the pendulum kick, very powerful and difficult to detect.

3.) Shuffle Kick
This is a long distance kick used by applying the standard shuffle to your lead kick. The forward momentum of this kick makes it an explosive addition to your arsenal. Be aware that a sidestep by your opponent can easily defend your shuffle kick. Due to its telegraphic qualities, use sparingly.

4.) Step And Shuffle Kick
The step increases your distance and the speed of your entry. This was referred to as a "forward burst" by Sigung Lee. For a faster initiation, sweep your lead hand upward. As your hand raises, swing your hips forward simultaneously, sliding your rear foot forward and exploding into your target. This is also a very telegraphic kick, so use caution.

Experiment by applying all your lead kicks to these four distances. The more versatile you are with your kicking skills, the better equipped you will be at controlling the distance.

PENDULUM FOCUS GLOVE DRILL

This drill is a great way to develop and improve your timing, balance, distance. and focus as well as the applicative skill of your pendulum kick.

You will need a partner and two focus gloves to begin. Place the focus glove on your right hands and face each other in a right lead On Guard position 2-3 feet out of kicking range. Hold the focus glove horizontal having the striking surface facing the floor at about groin level with your fingers pointing to the left. (For safety be sure not to hold the focus glove close to you.)

As you begin. pendulum toward your partner striking their focus glove with your lead upward snap kick 'Gin Tek' and pendulum back returning to your original position. Immediately upon your return hold your target (focus glove) in preparation as your partner duplicates your action kicking the target with their pendulum snap kick. Once you both feel confident continue as you did in the previous drill working 3 count repetitions. A total of 10 sets of 3 allows each partner the opportunity to both initiate and counter attack while providing a challenging workout routine.

JUN FAN GUNG FU

截拳道

To train the pendulum lead round kick "Nao Tek" hold the focus glove facing left in a vertical position directly in front of you at mid or head height and apply the 3 count concept. This is a great exercise to improve the focus of your thrusting kicks as well. To train the lead front kick 'Jik Tek' or lead side kick "Juk

Tek' hold the focus glove like a mirror directing it at your partner's midsection or head. Be sure to train both right and left lead kicks to balance skills. Later simply free feed the focus glove alternating the holds targeting different positions for your partner to spontaneously kick.

CHAPTER CONCLUSION

These are only some of the kicks found in Jun Fan, at the Kickboxing phase of development. Keep in mind that most kicks can be used both lead and rear. However, the lead kicks are generally more efficient because of their distance to the target. A major principle of "Jeet Kune Do" is to use the closest weapon to the nearest target.

KICKING KEY POINTS TO REMEMBER

1.) Be sure that your legs are warmed up and well stretched before you kick. Start out slow and build up the intensity as you progress thru your workout.

2.) Always stay balanced. Before, during, and after any kick or combination. Don't reach for the target or hyper-extend your joints. Use footwork to get into proper range.

3.) As in all phases of your "skill development," train with good form. Don't sacrifice form and balance for speed and power. Your speed and power will develop through application of proper form and balance.

4.) Breathe out as you kick and inhale after completion. Breathing is an important part of any martial art.

5.) Most kicks will be more effective if thrown below the horizontal perimeter of gates 1 and 2. and applied to gates 3, 4, 5, and 6.

6.) Don't chamber your kick, propel it straight to the target.

7.) An initial hand technique or feint will improve your success, if applied preceding your kick.

LESSON 8
JUN FAN TRAPPING

Bruce Lee's trapping was said to be one of the most remarkable areas of his fighting skills. Since most traditional styles of martial arts blocked with the lead hand and strike with the rear hand. Lee found that trapping the lead hand worked very well when applied to that structure., The attachment was relatively easy to obtain on the opponent's lead hand and once that arm was trapped the rear hand was rarely used to block, as it was in Lee's core art Wing Chun. Gaining an attachment is much like the crossing of swords when two fencers engage their blades.

Although this chapter focuses on the basics of hand immobilization, it is only a sliver of what actually encompasses the immobilization attack. An immobilization attack may be performed on any limb, the head, or any area of the body to restrict movement. For example, a foot trap is a very effective way to keep your opponent in range and restrict his kicking ability. when performing any close quarter simple or compound trap you should influence the body's position to compromise the adversary's balance and freedom to counter your attack. It is always important to cover the possibility of being snap kicked in the groin by checking the shin to immobilize the leg as you trap the upper body. The immobilization attack is one of the most difficult attacks to perform in the chaos of combat.

Trapping drills using the focus glove are integrated into the intermediate Jun Fan student's training. Drills such as the Jun Fan "ping chuie/gua chuie series" works the student in entering, punching, kicking, and trapping. In order for a student to be capable of this level of training I feel they must be proficient in each individual area first.

BASIC SLAPPING HAND TRAP & HIT-PAK SAO DA

The Pak Sao (as discussed in Chapter 3) is used as a key component in Jun Fan Trapping. The Pak Sao can be applied from an attachment or picked up "in flight" with either the lead or rear hand. An attachment is a "reference point" achieved thru an incidental or planned action where two limbs (yours and your opponent's) make contact and attach or stick momentarily.

This may happen initially or during an ABC or compound HIA applied by you or your opponent. A Simple trap is the application of a technique that immobilizes one limb. Where as a compound trap immobilizes both of the opponents arms allowing you in either case to attack an unguarded area or "open line".

HIGH OUTSIDE ATTACHMENT

As you attack or defend a high outside line (zone 2) you attach to your opponents limb. Using enough pressure to stick (not push thru) control the center line by occupying it and immediately slap (pak) your opponent's forearm with your rear hand, removing the obstruction as you strike. A skilled Jun Fan practitioner uses a relaxed heavy palm when paking. This adds a definite sting to your Pak Sao and a very brief motor skill dysfunction to your targeted arm making it hard to react.

You can use most lead hand attacks with pak sao as long as you are direct and immediate using forward pressure as you attack. Press using sticking energy to monitor the trapped arm, don't push their arm. Pushing the arm creates momentum allowing your opponent to move their arm or swing with the "Jao Sao" (running hand) to strike you by capitalizing on the energy you've provided.

1) GAINING AN ATTACHMENT WHEN YOUR PARTNER BLOCKS USING BIL SAO AND SWAYING BACK AWAY FROM THE ATTACK 2) TRAPPING THE ATTACHED LEAD WITH PAK SAO USING FORWARD PRESSURE

LOW OUTSIDE ATTACHMENT

This is similar to the previous technique though the pak sao is applied on a different line. As your opponent attempts to strike you. for example with a low jab "ping chuie", you will connect to his arm with a goang sao or low outside block. Once the attachment is made immediately Pak sao and strike to the head area.

Some of the most practical strikes for the low Pak Sao Da are the backfist "gua chuie", "saut sao" or chopping hand, the straight punch 'ichung chuie" or the finger jab "bil gee". Use extreme care when practicing the bil gee with a partner as it is extremely dangerous. I have my students tap the forehead lightly for purpose of safety.

1) DEFENDING THE LOW TO CONNECT THE ATTACHMENT 2) MONITOR THE LIMB AS YOU PAK SAO PREPARE TO SWING FORWARD 3) SHOOT YOUR LEAD ATTACK IMMEDIATELY WHEN THE LEAD HAND IS TRAPPED

LOW OUTSIDE TO HIGH OUTSIDE

This variation will come into effect in the event that your opponent's reaction is quick enough to default your low pak sao by them stepping back and blocking their high outside line with their lead hand. When this occurs you will be in the high outside reference point attachment. If so, immediately Pak sao da.

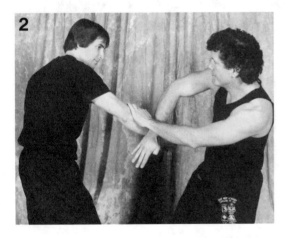

1) ATTACKING ON THE LOW LINE 2) AS THE FORWARD PRESSURE IS APPLIED THE PARTNER STOPS AND SLIDES 3) REMOVING THE FORWARD PRESSURE 4) IMMEDIATELY TRAP ON THE HIGH LINE

HIGH OUTSIDE OR INSIDE (IN FLIGHT)

This simple trap is similar in initiation to "'Lin Sil Die Da" simultaneous block/hit, however there are two major differences. As a straight line punch is thrown to zone 1 (high inside gate) you apply your Pak sao and stick to your attacker's arm. As you guide their punch forcing it down and clearing the way, you shoot out your attack over the Paking hand directly to the target. This can be done with the Rear Pak / Lead Strike or Lead Pak / Rear Strike methods. I personally prefer to Pak to the outside of my opponents arm as shown in the photos.

The inside (catch in flight Pak) is more difficult to perform requiring much more speed and timing. The in flight "Pak Sao Da" is a more applicable method for the quick puncher who snaps his punches out and retracts his punches immediately back into the guard position. Thru trial and error find what works for you. A boxer for example leaves little opportunity for an attachment, an in flight catch or trap or a stop punch or kick may be much more effective. The in flight application is also very useful at capturing your opponents arm in its chamber jamming it before it can strike, or capturing it in the chamber after an attack.

JUN FAN GUNG FU

1) PAKING THE JAB IN FLIGHT WITH NOY PAK SAO 2) ROCKING FORWARD SHOOTING DIRECTLY TO THE TARGET

PAK SAO WEDGE

The pak sao wedge will occur when your opponent blocks the strike from your "pak sao da" with enough force to push your attacking hand across their centerline. As this happens immediately shoot your straight punch or finger jab at their head area with your rear hand "wu sao" over your blocked arm to their open line.

As you do this maintain contact with both of their arms applying sliding energy with the use of your forearm as you "wedge" your rear hand attack directly to its target. Be sure to withdraw your lead hand back to the guard position to finish with a straight blast "jik chung chuie" or other ABC.

SEEKING THE PATH OF JEET KUNE DO

IF YOUR PAK SAO IS BLOCKED AND FORCED PAST CENTER, THE LINE IS OPEN FOR A WEDGED FOLLOW UP

PAK SAO DA/LOP SAO DA

The "pak sao da / lop sao da" can be applied after your opponent reacts to the initial "pak sao da" HIA in the same manner as above. In both the "pak sao wedge" and the "pak sao da / lop sao da" the opponent must parry your attempt to hit him with the pak sao da with enough force to push it across their centerline.

As you feel the energy from their parry, roll your striking arm into the "bong sao" position and grab their parrying hand and pull, using the cross hand grab "lin lop sao". As the parrying hand is secured roll your "boang sao" (referred to as swinging gate) over the top of their secured arm and strike while maintaining forward pressure with the elbow and forearm.

AS YOUR PARTNER PARRIES PAST YOUR CENTER, ROLL YOUR ARM WITH THEIR ENERGY – CROSS GRAB THE ARM LOPPING AS YOU STRIKE

PAK SAO DA / LOY PAK SAO DA

This variation of compound HIA is used against the opponent who; upon your initial "pak sao da" attack, uses only enough power to parry your strike to their centerline. This makes it illogical to attempt to "lin lop sao" as the energy is not sufficient enough for the "swinging gate bong sao" to roll across their centerline and the centerline is already open to a counter.

THREE BASICS OF THE LOY PAK SERIES ARE:

1.) "Bil gee" the throat area with your "wu sao" immediately when you feel your initial "pak sao da" strike is parried to their centerline. Directly after you score with the "bil gee", loy pak the inside of their "wu sao" (parrying hand) hard with the same hand while simultaneously striking with the other hand. Be sure to maintain forward pressure while using the elbow of your paking hand to pin the other hand as well.

2.) The second basic is almost identical to the first, but instead of striking the high line, you shoot your chung chuie into abdominal area. Immediately upon contact with the abdominal area "loy pak" their wu sao while once again simultaneously striking with your lead hand.

3.) The third basic is augmented upon the response of your opponent during the initial pak sao da. When you pak sao da, your opponent is unresponsive and your hit makes contact. Your opponent then attempts to punch with his rear hand to which you answer using "Tan Sao Da" to cut his energy or "Lie Sao Da" to pull his strike in as you deflect and hit.

Your follow up would be the same as #1 and #2 using the loy pak da as a final trapping blow. These can all be followed thru with an ABC, throw or take down and finishing hold if needed.

JUN FAN GUNG FU

截拳道

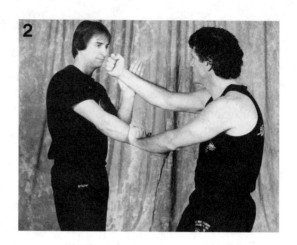

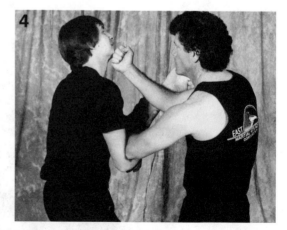

AS YOUR PARTNER PARRIES PAST YOUR CENTER, SHOOT OUT YOUR BILGEE TO THE THROAT AREA – IMMEDIATELY PAK AND STRIKE WHILE PRESSING FORWARD WITH YOUR ELBOW AND FOREARM

JUN FAN GUNG FU

WHEN THE PAK SAO IS PARRIED – THRUST YOUR STRAIGHT PUNCH TO THE BODY – LOY PAK THE BLOCKING HAND ONCE AGAIN WITH A SECOND STRIKE

SEEKING THE PATH OF JEET KUNE DO

AS YOUR PARTNER ATTEMPTS TO STRIKE, TAN DA CUTTING HIS ENERGY – FOLLOW UP WITH LOY PAK DA

LOY PAK SAO SERIES BASICS

1. PAK SAO DA TO LOY PAK SAO DA
2. PAK SAO DA TO CHUNG CHUIE, LOY PAK SAO DA
3. PAK SAO DA TO BIL GEE, LOY PAK SAO DA
4. PAK SAO DA TO TAN SAO DA, LOY PAK SAO DA
5. PAK SAO DA TO LIE SAO DA, LOY PAK SAO DA

JAO SAO – THE RUNNING HAND

Jao sao. "The running hand," is a very swift and deceptive component of the fundamental foundation of Jun Fan's trapping. Based on the principles of disengagement, forward energy and dissolving energy, "Jao Sao" can be predicated as either an offensive hand immobilization attack, a counter to pak sao da, or a counter to most defensive parries or obstructive limb attachments.

For the purpose of this chapter we will focus on 2 basic ways to use jao sao in detail.

We will begin with the "Pak Sao Jao Sao" commencing from the high outside reference point. Immediately upon contact with your opponents arm remove the obstructive ma sao attachment using noy pak sao (outside slapping hand). While disengaging your lead hand, swing it towards the opposite outside in a slapping motion to the side of your opponent's head.

The second method we will touch on is the application of Jao Sao as a counter for Pak Sao Da. As your opponent attempts to trap your hand and hit you using a right lead Pak Sao Da, flow with the energy of his trap and swing your hand, running it to the left side of his head in a slapping motion.

JUN FAN GUNG FU

As you do this be sure to parry his attempted strike or you may be hit first. Remember to relax as much as possible and execute the trap with smooth flowing energy. Listed below are a few of the basic reference points and routes used in the technical application of Jao Sao.

SEEKING THE PATH OF JEET KUNE DO

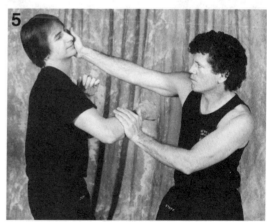

1 & 2) DISENGAGE YOUR LEAD HAND AS YOU PAK SAO YOUR PARTNERS ATTACHED LIMB 3) ROLL YOUR WRIST AND SWING YOUR HAND AROUND THE OBSTRUCTION 4) AS YOUR HAND RUNS CONTINUE TO PRESS THE IMMOBILIZATION 5) I PREFER TO USE THE PALM SLAP WHEN I JAO

JUN FAN GUNG FU

140

JAO SAO AS A COUNTER 1 & 2) AS YOUR PARTNER ATTEMPTS TO PAK SAO DA HINGE YOUR ARM TO LOW BONG SAO 3) SWING YOUR ARM USING HIS FORWARD PRESSURE TO HELP YOUR ARM FLOW TO THE TARGET 4) BE SURE TO MONITOR THE LEAD HAND ATTACK AS YOU COUNTER

BASIC JAO SAO REFERENCES

1. High Outside to Opposite High Outside
2. Mid (split) to High Outside
3. Low Outside to Opposite High Outside
4. Low Outside to High Outside to Opposite High Outside
5. Counter (for pak sao da)

CHI SAO – STICKING HANDS DRILL SERIES

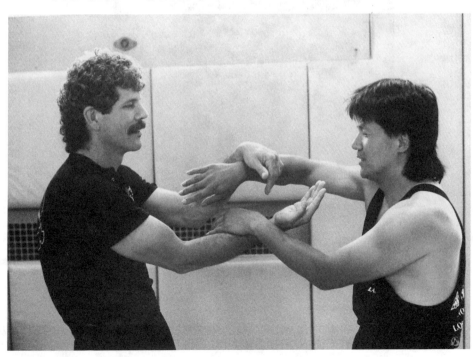

Although the task of learning "Chi Sao" from a book would be incomparably difficult from a technical aspect and nearly impossible from a tactile aspect, it cannot be overlooked as an important facet of the curriculum of the Jun Fan Gung Fu trapping method.

The major challenge in teaching "Chi Sao" is due to the character of the drills in their application and reception of tactile energy. One person must communicate the feel and flow of Chi Sao energy to another. In order for the student to become more proficient in the trapping phase of Jun Fan Gung Fu, I would recommend some personal instruction.

At minimum the Jun Fan Jeet Kune Do practitioner should have a basic knowledge of Chi Sao structure and practice. To accomplish this seek out a qualified wing chun or Jun Fan instructor. The majority of my Chi Sao training was given to me by Sifu Dan Inosanto of Los Angeles and Sifu Francis Fong of Atlanta, Georgia.

SIFU FRANCIS FONG TRAPPING ME WITH AMAZING SPEED AND ACCURACY FOR SEMINAR PARTICIPANTS AT THE EAST WEST ACADEMY

QUESTIONS ABOUT TRAPPING

Q. My brother does Amateur Boxing. He moves so quickly, I can't seem to trap his hand. Does trapping really work?

A. A boxer's structure makes trapping very difficult. When a boxer hits, they bring their hand right back to their head and usually follow up immediately with a combination. This structure is difficult to trap. Bruce Lee knew this and adapted Jun Fan's kickboxing to handle this problem. In some cases, the best you can achieve is to momentarily trap their punch in flight or capture it in the chamber.

Q. When I'm practicing trapping drills with my partner, it seems that my partner can always free his arm. Yet, when he traps me, I'm helpless. What's wrong?

A. Providing that your trap is basically being done correctly, it sounds as though possibly your distance is off. In order to trap effectively, you must apply constant forward pressure and close quickly as you trap offsetting your opponents balance while immobilizing one or both arms.

Q. Should my weight be on the balls of my feet or on my heels when I'm trapping?

A. Excellent question! Your weight should be up and agile on the balls of your feet when in kickboxing range, this allows you to move freely. Once you enter and initiate your hand and, or leg immobilization or move into a clinch to grapple your weight should lower onto your heels into a Wing Chun style stance as you move forward. This will help stabilize you by grounding your center of gravity.

" Don't think, Feel!"
Sigung Bruce Lee
From the movie "Enter the Dragon"

LESSON 9
JKD'S FIVE WAYS OF ATTACK DRILLS

Bruce Lee's contributions had a definite impact on the ways many people perceive and practice the martial arts today. Through his personal research and experience, Si-Gung Lee found many universal concepts and principles that he referred to as basic truths.

Lee was very much a pioneer of creative perceptions in the martial arts and often looked at things from what is referred to today as "Outside the Box". His belief that self improvement thru personal development and self knowledge were carried over to everything we did. He felt that self knowledge was the basis of Jeet Kune Do and that it held many keys to both success in martial arts and his personal life. He did whatever he felt would develop and improve him physically and psychologically. His research was timeless and flowed into many areas not investigated by traditional martial artists.

Because of his unique perception and exploratory mindset, Bruce Lee examined and realized the benefits of cross training, now a common training approach by martial artists today. Seeking the path to find the most effective and efficient ways to succeed. Lee searched for common thread techniques, concepts, principles and training methods from every fighting system, eastern or western in origin.

Some of the ideas used by Lee came from principles found in Western fencing. The stop hit attack, leading straight, beat attack and principle of timed attacks were just a few. He would use terms often used by fencers like engagement, disengage, parry, riposte, and cadence.

One of his many outstanding discoveries was that most types of attack fall into one of five distinct methods. The concept of the principles of "5 ways of attack" came about as a conclusion to three basic attacks found in European fencing. The simple direct and simple angular attack, the indirect attack or progressive indirect attack, and the attack by drawing were terms fond in classical fencing. the other two were thru obvious conclusion.

Here are a few examples of each:

SINGLE DIRECT ATTACK – S.D.A./S.A.A.

The most common attack is the single or simple direct attack or S.D.A. It's exactly the way it sounds; one, single offensive motion straight to the point. A few examples are: A lead jab, a low lead side kick, a rear round kick to the leg.

An S.A.A or single angular attack is a form of S.D.A. thrown from an angle by zoning, using the proper footwork.

The single direct attack can be applied as an exploratory technique or probe, used to test an opponent's reaction or create an opening. It can be used offensively or defensively, as a counter attack or stop hit.

SDA USED AS A STOP KICK COUNTER AGAINST A JAB

SDA USED AS A STOP KICK COUNTER AGAINST A ROUND KICK

SEEKING THE PATH OF JEET KUNE DO

AFTER DELIVERING A SDA TO INTERCEPT PARTNERS ROUND KICK – PARTNER FOLLOWS WITH A JAB – TIMING HIS ATTACK, SIDESTEP AND ANGLE YOUR LEAD STRAIGHT SAA

JUN FAN GUNG FU

SDA AS A STOP-HIT TIMED ATTACK BETWEEN THE PARTNERS JAB/CROSS. AS YOUR PARTNER JABS CATCH THE JAB – AS SOON AS YOU SEE THE CROSS COMING INTERCEPT WITH YOUR LEAD JAB

SDA USED AS A PROBE – AS YOUR PARTNER TRIES TO DELIVER A ROUND KICK – INTERCEPT THE ATTACK WITH A LEAD ROUND KICK TO HIS INNER THIGH – THIS DRILL WILL TEACH YOU TIMING, SPEED AND REACTION SKILLS

ATTACK BY COMBINATION – A.B.C.

An attack by combination is comprised of two or more offensive techniques applied in succession. Each one is meant to make contact. The offensive tools used in A.B.C. can be a combination of lead or rear hand and/or kicking techniques, elbow strikes, knees, head butts, etc. Practice your A.B.C.'s with accuracy and correct body mechanics.

Be careful not to abbreviate your body mechanics in order to speed through the combination. Always maintain quality and use movements that fit together naturally and flow smoothly. Maintain your guard by keeping your hands up or on center as appropriate. Combinations that don't require extreme sacrifices in your defense reduce your risk of being countered.

SEEKING THE PATH OF JEET KUNE DO

PARRY THE PARTNERS KICK TO THE MID SECTION WITH YOUR ELBOW – FOLLOW UP WITH A CROSS AND LEAD UPPERCUT

JUN FAN GUNG FU

截拳道

PARTNER JABS, CATCH THE JAB – PARRY HIS CROSS WITH YOUR LEAD HAND – AS HE HOOKS WITH THE LEAD STOP HIT WITH YOUR LEAD STRAIGHT PUNCH SIMULTANEOUSLY BLOCKING WITH YOUR LEFT – FINISH WITH A CROSS TO THE FACE

SEEKING THE PATH OF JEET KUNE DO

153

JUN FAN GUNG FU

AS YOUR PARTNER LEADS WITH A ROUND KICK, DEFEND BY LIFTING YOUR FRONT LEG UP. IMMEDIATELY FOLLOW UP WITH A ROUND KICK TO HIS INNER THIGH AND LEFT CROSS COMBINATION

PROGRESSIVE INDIRECT ATTACK – P.I.A.

A P. I.A. is comprised of a feint or uncommitted attack to one gate. which is designed to get a defensive reaction and create an opening. As the opening is created, the P.I.A. continues progressing to the real target. This is done in one smooth forward motion without withdrawing. Your first motion should be deep enough to gain distance toward your target, making it believable.

THE PRINCIPLE USES OF THE P.I.A. ARE:

a. To con the opponent whose defense is strong enough to defend against an S.D.A. or immobilization attack.

b. Bridge the gap for an A.B.C., H.I.A., grappling, or finishing blow.

A P.I.A. can be applied with the lead hand or elusive lead, or a combination

FAKE A LOW JAB TO PARTNERS MID SECTION – WITHOUT ANY PULLING BACK THE HAND REDIRECT YOUR STRIKE TO HIGH LINE HITTING BACKFIST

of hand and for kicking techniques. Although P.I.A. uses feints and disengagements, your "progressive indirect attack" must be executed in a continuous forward motion. To be effective, it should be preceded by a series of single attacks.

JUN FAN GUNG FU

截拳道

PIA TO ABC – LEAD WITH HIGH LINE JAB, AS YOUR PARTNER IS PARRYING YOUR STRIKE CHANGE IT TO A LOW JAB TO HIS MID SECTION – FOLLOW UP WITH A COMBINATION OF REAR CROSS AND LEAD BODY HOOK

SEEKING THE PATH OF JEET KUNE DO

157

JUN FAN GUNG FU

BRIDGE THE GAP BY FAKING A LEAD HIGH PUNCH – A SIMULTANEOUSLY HIT A LOW SIDE KICK – FOLLOW UP WITH LEAD STRAIGHT, REAR CROSS TO BODY AND LEAD UPPERCUT COMBINATION

ATTACK BY DRAWING – A.B.D.

An A.B.D. is a type of counter attack which uses a false opening to entice your opponent into launching an attack to that line. The intent is to create an opening in the attacker's defense and hit the opening before he can complete his action. As with all counter attacks, the keys to success are timing and distance. The distance must be adequate enough to make your opponent commit to your opening. As he steps in, time his attack! The success of "Attack By Drawing," depends largely on concealing your real intention of stop hitting or jamming the offensive action.

JUN FAN GUNG FU

截拳道

(SETUP TO STOP KICK DRILL) INVITING A LONG RANGE ATTACK BY OPENING THE BODY OUT OF KICKING RANGE. AS YOUR PARTNER SHUFFLES IN TO KICK, STOP THE KICK WITH A LEAD LEG OBSTRUCTION, BE SURE TO FOLLOW UP BEFORE YOUR PARTNER HAS TIME TO RECOVER HIS BALANCE, IN THIS CASE USING A LEAD STRAIGHT FOLLOW UP

SEEKING THE PATH OF JEET KUNE DO

截拳道

161

JUN FAN GUNG FU

截拳道

(USING AN EVASION DRILL) OPEN THE HIGHLINE, YOUR PARTNER LEADS WITH A JAB/CROSS – SNAP BACK FROM HIS JAB – AS SOON AS HE THROWS HIS CROSS BOB AND WEAVE UNDER THE ATTACK AND DELIVER A BODY SHOT AS YOU ENTER – SLIDE YOUR ARM UP CAPTURING HIS ARM AND NECK IN A TRIANGLE CHOKE. MOVE TO HIS BACK AND FINISH THE LOCK

SEEKING THE PATH OF JEET KUNE DO

(COMBINING BOTH PRINCIPLES DRILL) AS YOUR PARTNER JABS/CROSSES, SNAP BACK AWAY FROM THE JAB AND SHOULDER ROLL THE CROSS SIMULTANEOUSLY ATTACKING THE LEAD LEG TO STOP THE ATTACK. FOLLOW UP WITH A REAR CROSS

(HAND) IMMOBILIZATION ATTACK – H.I.A. OR I.A.

An H.I.A. is the application of an immobilizing technique or trap on an opponent's hand. arm. shoulder, leg, foot or head, as you or your opponent crash the line of engagement. Sometimes referred to as ABT or attack by trapping by Sifu Dan Inosanto.

Immobilization attacks can be set up, using any of the previous four ways of attack or while defending against your opponent's action. An H.I.A. may also occur incidentally in the midst of an attack, when you or your opponent meet an obstruction. We call this an attachment.

There are basically three ways to gain an attachment:

a. When you attack and your opponent defends.

b. When you engage upon defending your opponent's attack.

c. By throwing garbage. Throwing your hand out to gain an attachment, in order to force an opening.

Traps can be performed singularly or in combination. Trapping keeps the opponent from moving freely to defend or limits the tools available for defense or counter attack.

SEEKING THE PATH OF JEET KUNE DO

(TRAPPING TO GRAPPLING DRILL) JAB LOW TO GAIN AN ATTACHMENT WITH YOUR PARTNER – WHILE PAKING THE ARM SWING THE JAO SAO ACROSS THE NECK AND MOVE TO HIS BACK USING TRIANGLE FOOTWORK

JUN FAN GUNG FU

截拳道

(TRAP THE LEG DRILL) STEP AND ZONE AWAY FROM THE ROUND KICK CAPTURING YOUR PARTNER'S LEG – USE YOUR FOOTWORK TO CUT HIS LEG WITH YOUR SHIN – AS YOU STEP BEHIND HIS POST LEG, BACKFIST AND THROW – IMMEDIATELY TRAP THE LEG, CAPTURE BOTH LOWER LIMBS FOLLOWING WITH A RIGHT PUNCH – ARCH YOUR BACK AS YOU CRANK THE FIGURE FOUR ACHILLES LOCK – REMEMBER TO STOP WHEN YOUR PARTNER TAPS OUT

CHAPTER CONCLUSION

Although the five ways of attack are separately listed, they should be combined for a more effective use of each component, here are a few examples. A series of Single Direct Attacks are very useful as probes for creating openings for the ABC that finishes your opponent. Various single attacks, both direct and angular will also better convince the opponent that the first is real during a Progressive Indirect Attack sequence, they can also help to gain an attachment for a Hand Immobilization Attack. When your opponent disengages from your attachment, an Attack By Combination flurry can totally disorient that individual. The best way to use the SDA or SAA is as a broken time attack. Keep your single attacks crisp, economical, and efficient, hit on a direct line while keeping a tight cover. A single attack is an excellent tool for defense, whenever possible launch from a relaxed, poised position. At Attack by Drawing is basically the art of conning your opponent. The word "Con" comes from the word confidence. You must create a sense of confidence with them that they have a clear shot, then as you draw the attack act on it, with force and ferocity.

A technical progression I like to use is to probe my sparring partner's defense by using SDA's and SAA's applied in different tempos and broken timing with alive footwork and variable distancing. If I feel he is reacting well, I PIA as I crash his defense. If my PIA hits, I follow up with an Attack By Combination, if my opponent blocks, I attempt to attach and immobilize what ever I can, then follow up with an ABC or shoot for a take down.

The best way to train your 5 ways is by drilling, then experiment through sparring practice. Sparring is essential for your personal development in the martial arts. Sparring is application of your technical knowledge and ability. When you spar, work on your timing and repertoire, don't just compete with each other. When you compete as you practice, you limit what you will attempt to try. Because the competitive mentality does not want to fail, it therefore does not allow you to take chances and try new approaches, but relies on what has always worked. Spar with a win-win attitude. Sparring is play, when you spar play, but play seriously. Throw your ego to the side or better yet, leave it at the door. When you fight, fight to win, but sparring is not fighting.

Sifu Bruce Lee practiced what he preached, living by his own creed:
1. *"Jeet Kune Do utilizes all ways and is bound by none."*
2. *"Jeet Kune Do is finding the cause of your own ignorance."*
3. *"Using No Way as Way"* and *"Having no limitation as limitation."*
4. *"Absorb what is useful, reject what is useless and add what is specifically your own."*

It is important that a student in Jeet Kune Do have a good foundation in the Jun Fan method of Gung Fu before he expands, explores and "Absorbs What Is Useful" for his own personal system of Jeet Kune Do.
- Dan Inosanto

LESSON 10
JUN FAN AND JEET KUNE DO TERMINOLOGY

CHINESE TERMINOLOGY USED IN JUN FAN GUNG FU

BAI JONG – READY OR ON GUARD POSITION
BIL GEE – FINGER JAB
BIL SAO – THRUSTING HAND BLOCK
BONG SAO – RAISED ELBOW DEFLECTION
CHI SAO – STICKY HANDS
CHOAP CHUIE – KNUCKLE FIST
CHUM KIL – SEEKING TO BRIDGE THE GAP
CHUNG CHUIE – VERTICAL FIST
CHUNG JEOANG – CENTERLINE BLOCK
DA – STRIKE
DON CHI SAO – SINGLE HAND CHI SAO
DOAN SAO – LOW SLAPPING BLOCK
DUM TEK – STOMP KICK
FON SAO – TRAPPING HANDS
FOOK SAO – BENT ARM ELBOW IN BLOCK OR HOOKING HAND BLOCK
GIN CHUIE – UPPERCUT
GIN TEK – UPWARD SNAP KICK
GOANG SAO – LOW OUTER WRIST BLOCK OR LOW CUTTING ARM BLOCK
GO DA – MID (BODY) HIT
GUA CHUIE – BACK FIST
GUA TEK – INVERTED HOOK KICK
GUM SAO – PINNING HAND
HA DA – LOW HIT

HA PAK/DOAN SAO – LOW SLAP BLOCK
HA SO TEK – INVERTED SWEEP KICK
HAY, HEY – BEGIN
HOU – REAR
HOU TEK – BACK KICK
HUEN SAO – CIRCLING HAND
JANG – ELBOW
JAO SAO – RUNNING HAND
JOY – LEFT
JEEN – LEAD
JEET GEK – JAM WITH SHIN
JEET TEK – STOP KICK OR INTERCEPTING KICK
JEET QUE – INTERCEPTING BRIDGE
JEET KUNE – INTERCEPTING FIST
JIK CHUNG CHUIE – STRAIGHT BLAST
JIK JERN – STRAIGHT PALM
JIK TEK – STRAIGHT KICK
JIT TEK – SNAP KICK WITH TOE
JOAP HOP – GROUP TOGETHER
WOANG JERN – SIDE PALM
JUK TEK – SIDE KICK
JUN FAN – BRUCE LEE'S CHINESE NAME (MEANS RETURN AGAIN)
JUNE TEK – SPIN KICK
JUNG DA – MIDDLE HIT
JUT SAO – JERKING HAND
KAO SAO – SCOOPING BLOCK
KWOON – SCHOOL, GYM, INSTITUTE
LIE SAO – PALM UP PULLING HAND TAN SAO
LIN LOP SAO – CROSS GRABBING HAND
LIN SIL DIE DA – SIMULTANEOUS BLOCK AND HIT
LOOK SAO – ROLUNG HANDS DRILL
SUNG LOON SAO – HIGH HORIZONTAL ARM BLOCK
LOP SAO – OUTSIDE GRABBING HAND
LOY – INSIDE
LOY PAK SAO – INSIDE (OF THE ARM) SLAPPING HAND
MON SAO – INQUISITIVE HAND
NOY – OUTSIDE
NOY PAK SAO – OUTSIDE (OF THE ARM) SLAPPING HAND
NOY PAK/LOY DA – SPLIT ENTRY

NAO CHUIE – HOOK PUNCH
NAO TEK – HOOK OR ROUND KICK
PAK SAO – SLAPPING HAND BLOCK
PING CHUIE – HORIZONTAL FIST
SIFU – INSTRUCTOR, TEACHER, FATHER
SI-GUNG – YOUR INSTRUCTOR'S TEACHER
SI-HING – YOUR SENIOR IN RANK (MALE)
SI JA – YOUR SENIOR IN RANK (FEMALE)
SI MO – WIFE OF YOUR TEACHER, FEMALE TEACHER, MOTHER
SIJO – FOUNDER OF THE STYLE, SYSTEM OR METHOD
SOE GERK – FOOT SWEEP
SUNG DA – HIGH HIT
SUT – KNEE
SAUT SAO – CHOPPING HAND
TAN SAO – PALM UP BLOCK
WOANG PAK – SIMULTANEOUS RISING PARRY STRAIGHT PUNCH
WU SAO – PROTECTING HAND
YOW – RIGHT

TERMINOLOGY USED IN JEET KUNE DO

ABSORB – LEARN AND RETAIN AS KNOWLEDGE
APPLICATION – ABILITY TO USE YOUR KNOWLEDGE SPONTANEOUSLY

ATTACKS – DIFFERENT TYPES

COMPOUND ATTACK – OFFENSIVE ACTION THAT INCLUDES ONE OR MORE FEINTS BEFORE THE REAL ATTACK

PRIMARY ATTACKS – 3 WAYS TO APPLY

1. **PACE** – USING SUPERIOR SPEED, TIMING AND ACCURACY WITH NO ATTEMPT TO DISGUISE YOUR ATTACK
2. **FRAUD** – DECEIVE AN OPPONENT BY FAKING AN ATTACK ON ONE LINE AND UPON DRAWING A REACTION, ATTACKING AN OPEN LINE
3. **FORCE** – ATTACKING A CLOSED LINE WITH SUFFICIENT FORCE TO OPEN IT.

SECONDARY ATTACKS – 3 TYPES

1. **ATTACK ON PREPARATION** – AN ATTACK BEFORE AN OPPONENT CAN

MOVE.
2. **ATTACK ON DEVELOPMENT** – ATTACKING MIDWAY DURING AN OPPONENT'S ACTION.
3. **ATTACK ON COMPLETION** – ATTACKING WHEN AN OPPONENT IS AT FULL EXTENSION.

5 WAYS OF ATTACK – THE FIVE FUNDAMENTAL WAYS TO APPLY AN ATTACK

1. **S.D.A.** – SINGLE (simple) DIRECT ATTACK: ONE OFFENSIVE MOTION STRAIGHT TO THE POINT.
S.A.A. – SINGLE (simple) ANGULAR ATTACK: SINGLE ATTACK AT AN ANGLE
2. **A.B.C.** – ATTACK BY COMBINATION: TWO OR MORE HAND AND/OR FOOT ATTACKS IN SUCCESSION, COULD ALSO BE ELBOW, KNEE, HEAD BUTT, ETC...
3. **H.I.A.** – HAND IMMOBILIZATION ATTACK (A.B.T. – ATTACK BY TRAPPING): TRAPPING OR RETAINING A BODY PART; ARM, FOOT, LEG HEAD, ETC. TO KEEP IT FROM MOVING.
4. **P.I.A.** – PROGRESSIVE INDIRECT ATTACK: FAKING AN ATTACK TO ONE LINE OR GATE AND CHANGING TO ANOTHER LINE WHILE PROGRESSING IN. WITHOUT WITHDRAWING.
5. **A.B.D.** – ATTACK BY DRAWING: CREATING A FALSE OPENING BY LEAVING AN AREA UNPROTECTED WITH THE SPECIFIC PURPOSE OF COUNTERING.

ATTRIBUTE – A QUALITY OR CHARACTERISTIC INHERENT (TO BE DEVELOPED) IN A PERSON

BEAT ATTACK – A SHARP, CRISP BLOW TO THE ARM TO OPEN A LINE FOR ATTACK

BRIDGING – SLIDING ENERGY THAT DEFLECTS A PUNCH (USUALLY WHILE COUNTERING.)

BRIDGING THE GAP – SAFELY CLOSING THE DISTANCE BETWEEN YOU AND YOUR OPPONENT DURING YOUR ATTACK.

BROKEN RHYTHM – SUDDENLY BREAKING THE RHYTHM BETWEEN YOU AND YOUR OPPONENT BY STALLING, FEINTING, SLIGHT HESITATION AND TIMED HITS OR HALF BEATS.

CENTERLINE – AN IMAGINARY VERTICAL LINE DOWN THE CENTER OF THE BODY DIVIDING IT INTO TWO HALVES.

A CONCEPT – AN IDEA, A THOUGHT DRAWN FROM A SPECIFIC.

COUNTER – RESPONDING TO YOUR OPPONENT'S ATTACK WITH AN ATTACK.

CRISPY STUFF – FAST, CRISP S.D.A.'S, A.B.C.'S OR H.I.A.'S

CRASH – JAM AN ATTACKING LINE WHILE CLOSING THE GAP.
CUTTING THE TOOL – USING FORCE TO CUT INTO AN ATTACKING LIMB AND DEFLECTING IT WHILE YOU COUNTER.
DISSOLVING – REDIRECTING YOUR OPPONENT'S ATTACK FORCE AWAY DEFENSIVELY.
DRAWING – DRAWING IS CLOSELY ALLIED TO FEINTING. WHERE AS IN FEINTING AN OPENING IS CREATED, IN DRAWING A PART OF YOUR DEFENSE IS LEFT UNPROTECTED TO GET A SPECIFIC REACTION AND COUNTER IT.
ECONOMY OF MOTION – USING MINIMUM EFFORT AND MOVEMENT TO GAIN MAXIMUM EFFECT.
ENTRY – A SINGLE ATTACK OR SERIES OF ATTACKS OR FEINTS USED TO CLOSE THE DISTANCE.
EVASION – USING MOTION TO AVOID AN ATTACK.
FEINTING – USING YOUR HANDS, FEET, EYES. OR BODY TO DECEIVE AN OPPONENT CREATING AN OPENING.
FIGHTING MEASURE – DISTANCE MAINTAINED BETWEEN YOU AND YOUR OPPONENT.
FLOW – TO MOVE SMOOTHLY WITH UNBROKEN CONTINUITY.
GAINING AN ATTACHMENT – MAKING BODILY CONTACT IN ORDER TO CONTROL, DISRUPT, TRAP OR READ AN OPPONENT'S MOTION.
GARBAGE – LEADING WITH A TECHNIQUE WITH THE PURPOSE OF GAINING A REACTION OR ATTACHMENT.
JAMMING – SMOTHERING AN ATTACK BEFORE IT CAN GAIN MOMENTUM.
J.K.D. – JEET KUNE DO: THE WAY OF THE INTERCEPTING FIST
KNOWLEDGE – AGCUMULATION OF PREVIOUSLY LEARNED MATERIAL
LOCKING – IMMOBILIZING AND APPLYING PRESSURE AGAINST A JOINT.
A PRINCIPLE – A RULE, A BASIC TRUTH
PROBE – USING INVESTIGATIVE TECHNIQUES TO EXPLORE & MANIPULATE YOUR OPPONENT'S ACTIONS.
QUALITIES – MENTAL AND PHYSICAL ATTRIBUTES
REACTION TIME – REACTION TIME IS THE TIME GAP BETWEEN A STIMULUS AND A RESPONSE.
REVERSAL – A MOVE THAT REVERSES THE SITUATION, GIVING YOU THE ADVANTAGE.
SENSITIVITY TRAINING – TRAINING TO INCREASE YOUR SENSITIVITY TO MOTION DURING CONTACT. USED TO IMPROVE YOUR REACTION TIME.
STICKING ENERGY – MAINTAINING CONTACT WITH AN OPPONENT BY STICKING TO AN ARM OR LEG.
STOP-HIT – A STOP-HIT IS A TIMED HIT MADE AGAINST THE ADVERSARY AT

THE SAME TIME HE IS MAKING AN ATTACK.
TACTICS – STRATEGIES USED TO GAIN THE ADVANTAGE.
TELEGRAPHING – MAKING AN UNNECESSARY MOTION SIGNALING YOUR INTENTIONS
TOOLS – YOUR OFFENSIVE AND DEFENSIVE FUNCTIONAL REPERTOIRE OF WEAPONS
TRANQUILIZER – AN INITIAL HIT, BUMP, DISTRACTION OR DISABLING TECHNIQUE USED AS A PREFIX TO A COUNTER.
VISUALIZATION – THE ABILITY TO PICTURE SOMETHING IN YOUR MIND'S EYE.

CONCLUSION:
OVERALL TRAINING TIPS

1.) Partner training is very important. Without the interaction of a living, responsive person, you can only develop to a point. Work with your partner, not against him or her. Human interaction helps us grow.

2.) Although this book can guide you, it is recommended that you find a qualified, certified instructor in "Jun Fan and the Art and Philosophy of Jeet Kune Do" to continue your training and personal development. To quote Sifu Dan Inosanto: "One professor can't teach all subjects. I admire Bruce Lee saying, you've got to go to the experts!"

3.) Plan a regular training schedule. A time when you or you and a partner can work out. Keep to your schedule whenever possible. Two to three times a week for one to two hours is essential to your skill development. Any less and your progress will be slow.

4.) To achieve optimum results practice skill exercises in repetitions of at least 10 or more on each side. If you find your development is slow in one area, concentrate a little more on that area until it improves. Practice with your "focus" on what you are doing at that moment. Don't be distracted by other thoughts.

5.) Cross train to balance and complement your martial arts training with other physical fitness methods. Calisthenics, weight training, jogging, jumping rope, and biking are just a few. A good strength training program will make remarkable improvements in your personal development and lessen your potential for injury in everything you do. Stay on the "cutting edge" through personal research and development. Seek out the advice of a professional and personally research to discover your specific areas of need.

6.) Eat a well balanced diet with lots of complete carbohydrates, proteins and plenty of water. As an athlete you will require more protein than you realize. Always drink plenty of clean, pure water before, during and after your workouts. Water is an essential component of your physiology, so stay hydrated. Avoid junk foods and foods loaded with fat and sugar. Good nutrition is essential to the development of any athlete.

FACT: Bruce Lee injured his back causing damage to his sacral nerve in 1970. The injury was due to overtraining and lifting too heavy during "Good Mornings", a weight training exercise, not during a fight as many people believe. Although doctors told him he would not be able to continue his lifestyle in the martial arts, through determination he fully recovered and went on to star in four and a half films made between 1971 and 1973.

FACT: Did you know that Bruce Lee used the focus glove for martial arts training as far back as 1962? In fact, it was Bruce Lee who popularized its use in the martial arts.

FACT: Bruce Lee trained on a 300lb heavy bag to improve his kicking power.

FACT: Bruce Lee was far from being genetically perfect, as most people believe. Bruce Lee wore contact lenses and actually failed his physical exam in 1963 and was deemed physically unacceptable by the US Army Draft Board.

FACT: Bruce Lee was introduced to the football shield for kicking by student Dan Inosanto. At first, he rejected the idea, but within a few days he had developed a series of drills and the kicking shield became a mainstay of Jun Fan Gun Fu Jeet Kune Do training. Today there is a shield in almost every martial arts school in the USA.

FACT: Bruce Lee was one of the first Chinese Gung Fu teachers in the United States to teach non-chinese. Si-gung Lee did not allow racial discrimination to enter into his choice of who he wanted to teach. He chose to see people as individuals, and regardless of what the chinese community at that time wanted he stood his ground, even though he was challenged to fight as an ultimatum to stop teaching people other than those of Chinese descent.

IN CONCLUSION

The format of this book is set up as a developmental progression, in the style of a school text book. What I have done is organize and laid out a fundamental foundation of some of the technical framework of Jun Fan Gung Fu on a basic level. This book is also meant to help prepare the reader for further advancement and lay the groundwork for future volumes.

All martial arts are developmental in nature, and a student must have a strong foundation in order to grow. Although learning a martial art from a book is challenging and any book is really best used in conjunction with other learning mediums, such as video's training with a qualified instructor, and of course self study through practice.

Learning on any level is the accumulation of knowledge from the gathering of data. However, to really know how to use your knowledge and apply it skillfully can only be achieved through practice, persistence and repetition. The true process of learning occurs inside the individual as they digest the material and make it their own. This is the Jeet Kune Do concept of self-knowledge through self discovery. You can read all about the fundamentals of swimming and this will give you a greater understanding of the subject, but you need to get into the water in order to swim, then you need to teach your body how to perform the mechanics it takes to swim.

I would like to say to those of you who are seeking the path, thank you for taking the time and interest to improve yourself by reading this book. Always keep an open mind and a compassionate spirit, continue to believe in your self, keep working to achieve your goals, learn and train with a passion, and stay on that path of never ending improvement. Remember, repetition is the mother of skill!

Kevin R. Seaman

KEVIN SEAMAN'S VIDEOS

**Jun Fan Gung Fu – Concepts and Principles of Jeet Kune Do – Vol 1.
Seeking the Path.**

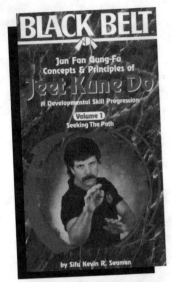

- The fundamental structure and foundation of Bruce Lee's Jun Fan Gung Fu.
- Evasive footwork and mobility that made Bruce Lee famous.
- Basic Body Mechanics that develop Jun Fan's explosive power.
- Jun Fan's powerful kicking techniques.

$29.95 +Handling. VHS.

**Jun Fan Gung Fu – Concepts and Principles of Jeet Kune Do – Vol 2.
Basic Tool Development.**

- Introduction to JKD's 5 ways of attack.
- How to develop and apply devastating hand combinations and keep them razor sharp.
- More on Jun Fan's kicking techniques.
- Continued from Volume 1 – Developmental Skills essential to your progression in Jun Fan Gung Fu.

$29.95 +Handling. VHS.

Both the above videos are available from:
Blackbelt Magazine Video or
Kevin Seaman c/o East West Martial Arts Academy, 255 Tompkins Street, Cortland, NY 13045.
Phone: (607) 756-4961.
www.ewmaa.com